PLANTING MEMORIES

PLANTING MEMORIES

A Settler's Life on the Sogeri Plateau

ANTHEA MATLEY

SEVENPENS

Planting Memories
Copyright © Anthea Matley, 2024

First published 2024

Published by Sevenpens Publishing
Harcourt, VIC 3453, Australia
http://www.sevenpenspublishing.com

National Library of Australia Cataloguing-in-Publication data:
Creator: Matley, Anthea 1957 – author
Title: *Planting Memories*
ISBN 978-0-9954144-2-6
Subjects: Matley, Anthea 1957 – Biography, History, Family History, Memoir

Front Cover: Photograph of Culver and Margaret Matley
Photographer unknown. Photo courtesy of Anthea Matley's collection
Back Cover: Photo of 'Snake Road up to Rouna falls, 2018' by Anthea Matley
Cover Design: Katherine Seppings
Book Design: Katherine Seppings

Printed by: Lightning Source/Ingram Spark

This book is part-memoir, part creative non-fiction and part biography.
The work depicts actual events in the life of the author and the lives of
her parents as truthfully as recollection permits and has been verified by
historical research, the facts of which are believed to be true but some
cannot be fully substantiated. Occasionally, dialogue consistent with the
character or nature of the person has been created.

Swimming in Eilogo Creek, 1963

About the Author

Anthea Matley was born in Port Moresby and grew up on a rubber plantation on the Sogeri Plateau, Papua New Guinea, immigrating to Australia in 1968.

Anthea obtained a Diploma of Professional Writing and Editing through the Kangan Institute, Bendigo, Victoria. She studied part-time while revegetating a forty-acre property at Faraday.

As part of her course work, Anthea assisted in producing and self-publishing an anthology of students' writing. In 2014, again with a team, she produced and published *Kidnapped by Time*, a history of the Faraday area.

Anthea has written short stories and poetry, and *Planting Memories* is her first creative non-fiction book. It took five years of research, writing, and a revisiting of her childhood home in Papua New Guinea.

She now lives in Elphinstone, central Victoria.

Matley family at Eilogo, 1964

Contents

Culver's Memories

Margaret's Story

Preface

I was born in Papua New Guinea on a plantation called Mororo, nestled within the rainforest and high fertile plains of the Sogeri Plateau. My father, apart from his army service during the Second World War, spent his whole working life as a settler-planter on the Mororo and Eilogo rubber plantations. During this time he met my mother, and together they built a home and garden and raised five children, of which I am the third. They learned Motu, the local language, and made close friends there.

When we left Papua New Guinea in 1968, I was eleven years old and unaware of the political and social changes that were taking place. I didn't understand that we would never be returning. As an adult looking back, I realised those early years of my upbringing were unique, and I wanted to record, mainly for my children and grandchildren, what it was like during that period of my childhood.

If you are born and raised in a place you loved as a child, that place holds a special connection for you as a part of your identity. Those pleasurable childhood memories might be mixed with sadness, anger and confusion at the changes that ripped you from your childhood home. I think it is natural to want to revisit that particular place as an adult. It was certainly true in my case. I had always longed to return to the country of my birth and to see Mororo and Eilogo again. I didn't expect things to have stayed the same, but I wanted to be reminded of how things were.

My parents preferred to let the past lie undisturbed and were vehemently against any of their children going back, saying, 'It won't be the same. Better to keep the good memories.'

They didn't understand my yearning to return. I accepted the political and cultural changes as necessary, but the 1950s and 1960s had been a wonderful time for me. I just wanted to see my 'homeland' again, for myself.

In early 2018, I ordered a book through an online bookstore specialising in the Pacific area. Then I received a phone call from Bill McGrath who owned the bookshop. He had recognised my surname, Matley, which is not a common one in Australia.

'I decided to ring you because I knew a Culver Matley. Would you, by chance, be related to him?'

I felt a tingle go down my spine.

Our long telephone conversation touched on three years of Bill's life between 1959 and 1961, when he worked as a surveyor in the Eilogo River Valley and on the Sogeri Plateau. It was a joy for him to remember the many wonderful people who had made him so welcome. He particularly remembered how kind my parents were when he was camping on the banks of the Eilogo River, surveying land that had been requisitioned for the Sirinumu Dam project.

I took this chance phone call and conversation with Bill as a sign that I had to go back to Papua New Guinea. Consequently, it set me on my path to record the history of my family's time there, beginning in 1935 when my father, Culver Matley, at the age of twenty-one, travelled from the bleak, rural plains of Canada to the tropical rainforest of the Sogeri Plateau north of Moresby.

Volunteers 2nd Kent   *a.J.M.*

Arthur (Jack) Matley Volunteer
2nd Kent Garrison Artillery, 1900

Timeline of Events

Matley Family Background

1865   James Matley (1865-1903) marries Lucy Skinner (1838-1899), London, England

1870   James moves to Bramshott, East Hampshire, where he becomes a coachman

Children:

1866   Frank Robert Matley

1869   Lucy Matley

1870   Charlotte Matley

1872   James William Matley (jnr)

1873   Henry Culver Matley

1875   Catherine Sophia Matley

1878   Archibald Louis Matley

1881   Arthur John (Jack) Matley

Jack Matley (1881-1958)

1881   Arthur John (Jack) Matley born

1900   Joins Second Kent Garrison as a volunteer

1903   Canadian emigration office established in London

1904   Martha's mother, Lucy Parfect dies

1905   Martha Parfect and Jack Matley marry

1906   Emigrate to Brandon, Manitoba, Canada

1906   Purchases 60 acres near Punnichy, Saskatchewan, Canada

1907	Built their house, broke and cropped ground, bought two cows
1908-9	Broke and cropped more land
1910	Bought eight more cows; homestead patent issued
1913	Family travels to Reading, England – Martha's father (Arthur Skinner) dying (Dec)
1914	WW1; travel back to Canada by sea (Jul)
1915	Enlists in Canadian Expeditionary Force; serves in France
1918	Injured in accident (Sep); 3 months in hospital, England
1918	Sent home to Canada (Dec)

Children:

1906	Francis William Matley born in Brandon (Sep)
1909	Mary Matley
1912	Arthur Matley (Dec)
1914	Culver Matley born in Reading, England (Feb)
1929	Saskatchewan's drought begins
1931	Crops fail
1932	Good crops but poor returns
1934	Dust storms and drought

Culver Matley (1914-1990)

1935	Sails from Vancouver to Samarai, Papua (Sep)
1935	Works on Waigani plantation, Papua
1936	Travels to work on Mororo Plantation (Mar)
1939	WW2 announced
1940	Enlists with 3rd Division Army Field Workshops

Culver Matley War Record

28/11/1940	Enlistment; general details depot, Sydney
2/12/1940	Joins 68 Light Aid Detachment, Liverpool
27/12/1940	Embarked on *Kantara*
3/02/1941	Disembarked in Egypt
25/04/1941	Graded as Group 3 Driver Mechanic
1/08/1941	Appointed Lance Corporal
23/09/1941	Accidentally injured at Aleppo. Small lacerated wound at leg above knee. Court of enquiry was not needed
17/03/1942	Embarked on *Glen Park*, Middle East
25/04/1942	Disembarked in Adelaide
3/05/1942	Admitted to 105 General Hospital with pyrexia, a persistent fever later diagnosed as malaria and transferred to X list. This recorded him as being absent from regular duties with just cause
22/05/1942	Discharged from 105 General Hospital and returned to unit
9/06/1942	Admitted, again, to 105 General Hospital with malaria and transferred to an X list.
13/06/1942	Discharged from 105 General Hospital and returned to unit
5/02/1943	Transferred to ANGAU (Australian New Guinea Administrative Unit) to carry out civilian duties
13/03/1946	Discharged – being required for employment in an essential occupation

| 1946 | Returns to Mororo to assist in rubber production |
| 1947 | Marries Margaret Anderson, Horsham, Australia (Jan) |

Margaret Matley, nee Anderson (1919-2007)

1919	Born in Horsham, Australia
1942	Joins RAAF Nursing Service (Jul)
1945	Arrives Port Moresby (Jan)
1945	Meets Culver Matley (Jul)
1945	Japanese surrender (Aug)
1945	Flies back to Australia (Nov)
1947	Marries Culver Matley, Horsham, Australia (Jan)

Culver and Margaret Matley

1947	Live at Mororo, PNG, Culver managing Mororo
1949	Margaret's sister, Mary, visits (Jun)
1951	CWA forms
1953	First agricultural show
1953	Planters' Association reformed
1954	US nuclear test on Eniwetok Atoll in the Marshall Islands
1956	Prince Philip visit
1957	Culver flies to Canada (Aug)
1957	Ian Loudon, manager of Eilogo, dies (Nov)
1958	Move to Eilogo to manage both Eilogo and Mororo Plantations
1958	Culver's father, Jack Matley, dies
1959	Catalina Plantation liquidated
1959	Land requisition begins for Sirinumu dam
1962	Indonesia lands troops in West Irian

1962	Agricultural show moves to Moresby
1963	Sirinumu dam opens
1965	Playing cards banned
1966	UN votes for Australia to set a date for PNG independence
1967	Culver resigns as Manager of Eilogo Estate Limited
1968	Family moves to Horsham, Australia
1969	Culver's mother, Martha Matley, dies
1971	Margaret's father, David Anderson, dies
1972	Margaret's mother, Florence Anderson, dies

Children:

1948	Beth, Horsham, Australia
1952	Christina, Port Moresby PNG
1957	Anthea, Port Moresby PNG
1959	John, Port Moresby PNG
1961	Sonya, Port Moresby PNG

| 1990 | Culver Matley dies, Victoria, Australia |
| 2007 | Margaret Matley dies, Victoria, Australia |

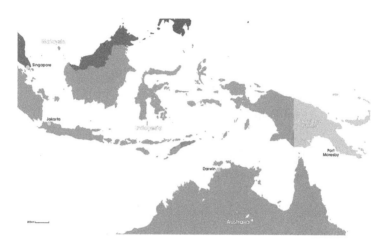

Indonesia, PNG, Australia

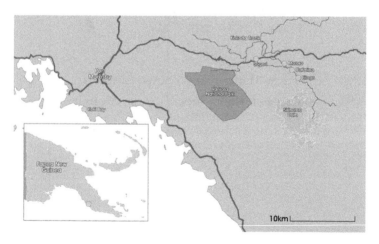

The Sogeri Plateau, PNG

Introduction

The Sogeri Plateau sits among the rising bluffs and foothills of the Owen Stanley Range, about fifty-six kilometres north-east of Port Moresby. The range lies on a division of continental plates. Because of its altitude (with mountains up to 3,800 metres high) and rainforest climate, it provides a rich habitat for endemic species including birds of paradise, bowerbirds, and finches. Wallabies, snakes, rats, and numerous species of butterflies are plentiful.

The vegetation varies from savanna to monsoon forest, lowland rainforest, cloud forest, grasslands and subalpine herbs. Varirata National Park covers one thousand hectares of the plateau. From the park's elevation of about eight-hundred metres you can view Port Moresby and the coast.

The Koiari and Orokaiva peoples are the Papuan owners of the region who leased land to the plantation companies to grow crops such as rubber. They now supplement their subsistence economy with income from tourism; mainly visitors hiking the Kokoda Track.

The story of rubber production in Papua New Guinea (PNG) is one of hardship and varying success, and in the latter half of the twentieth century, of failure. The plantations mentioned in this book were on negotiated ninety-nine-year leases of Koiari land. In 1903, eight acres, or 3.25 hectares, of Para rubber plants were planted at Sogeri and another two hectares the following year. These proved very successful and in

1906 the Australian Government actively encouraged the new industry and arranged the importing of rubber seeds.

The settlers on these plantations came from Australia. They would have been familiar with, or had some idea of, plantation life as found in Queensland and other tropical countries such as Fiji, Malaya or Sri Lanka (formerly Ceylon). However, on arriving in Papua after adjusting to the hot, humid climate, clearing the forest and managing local labour, they then had to face the reality of the land they had chosen. They expected that Papua would one day resemble those other countries which seemed prosperous. The Australian Government made substantial grants to Papua to encourage the development of government experimental plantations. Private enterprises followed this show of faith by also planting rubber.

The rubber industry of Papua was well established by the end of the First World War. In the 1920s, rubber plantations produced between six hundred and eight hundred tonnes of rubber per year and all the rubber produced was shipped to Australia. The price of raw rubber fluctuated widely. Before the Second World War the price was low, but during the war rubber became valuable.

The Japanese invasion of Papua New Guinea began in July 1942 as part of their broader Pacific campaign. Japanese forces rapidly advanced through the northern coast of Papua New Guinea, capturing strategic locations such as Rabaul and Lae. Their ultimate objective was to capture Port Moresby, and to achieve this they embarked on an overland push along the Kokoda Track towards Port Moresby.

The Australian forces, initially outnumbered and ill-prepared, forced the Japanese to retreat. By early November 1942, the Japanese had been effectively driven out of the area, after coming within about 48 kilometres of the Sogeri Plateau.

Most plantations had been evacuated or were out of production. However, the Australian New Guinea Administrative Unit (ANGAU) maintained the output of several plantations to keep up rubber production for the war effort.

Until the Second World War, the territory of Papua was administered separately from New Guinea. After 1945, Papua and New Guinea were combined under an administrative union. Australia had entered into a trusteeship agreement with the United Nations to govern Papua as part of an Australian territory, while being responsible to the United Nations for control of New Guinea. The two regions were now called the Territory of Papua and New Guinea, administered as a single unit from Port Moresby.

PNG obtained independence from Australia in 1975. Between 1975 and 1980 the PNG Government bought six plantations on the Sogeri Plateau on behalf of the traditional Koiari landholders. Eilogo, where I lived, was one of them. With the help of the National Plantations Management Agency, the hope was that the rubber industry could be rebuilt. The six plantations were combined under the Sogeri Rubber Development Corporation and were provided with experts in the rubber industry from Malaysia to assist. Since then, due to low prices for rubber and the decline in value of the PNG kina against foreign currencies, returns have barely covered operating costs. Many village people have drifted to the larger towns searching for work and a better life.

Many people assume the plantation system exploited the PNG people and that, during the colonial period, the planters profited from that exploitation. This isn't true. The same working conditions, and health and safety issues, applied to the planters and to the local employees alike. The planters did not become wealthy—they became casualties of the time's political, economic and cultural changes. However, the common experience of settling and working there did create within the planter community a shared sense of identity, destiny and group loyalty.

Portarlington

On a late winter afternoon, I watched my father, Culver, from the upstairs window of my parents' brick veneer home in Portarlington. He was standing in front of a 44-gallon drum he'd placed in the backyard orchard, far enough away so the flames from the fire couldn't scorch the delicate citrus leaves of the orchard.

While my mother, Margaret, rattled cups in the sink I had noticed my father in the backyard. My father's hands trembled as he reached for a folder from the high stack beside one of two plastic chairs. Opening the folder, he dropped the papers into the fire. Flames rose, licked at his hands, leaping and sparking. He stepped back, waiting for them to die down before feeding them more pages. He leant on his walking stick, staring at the fire, and in the glow of the yellow flames I could see his tired face, lined and grey.

'What's he up to?' I asked.

'You can go and ask him yourself,' my mother replied.

I walked at a brisk pace down the stairs and out to the fire.

'What are you doing, Dad?'

'I'm burning old documents. Stuff no one would be interested in reading.'

I couldn't believe what he was saying.

'There might be something I'd be interested in.'

'I doubt it,' he said. 'There's nothing here that would interest you.'

'I'd like to be the one to decide.'

'Nope.'

I knew I wouldn't be able to stop him.

'Could you tell me some of your stories, memories, as you're burning those folders?' I asked.

He finally turned to look at me with his weary eyes and nodded.

'Can I use my tape recorder? In case I forget.'

Another nod.

'What's in those folders? Are they important?'

He shook his head. 'No, just old files. I'm clearing the decks so no one else is burdened with them when I'm gone.'

I knew what he meant by that. He would only take the chemotherapy drugs long enough to stay alive so he could settle his affairs and teach my mother how to manage the household accounts. I knew that my chance to learn about my father's early life would be fleeting.

'What are you two up to?' asked Mum, finally appearing from the house.

'I'm going to revisit the past—and Anthea wants some of my reminiscences—for posterity. Come and join us,' replied Culver, who had stopped feeding the fire and was staring contemplatively at a yellowed document.

'Mum, would you help tell the story?' I asked.

'Yes,' she said, 'though it's not very interesting, and you know most of it already.'

And so, during my journey of discovery over the next few months, I found out details about my parents I hadn't known before, and the fragments I did know about, fell into place.

Culver's Memories

Culver in hockey gear, Punnichy, Canada, 1930s

Early Life in Canada
1905–1935

Punnichy, Saskatchewan, Canada 1930s

I grew up in Punnichy, a little prairie town in Saskatchewan, a huge, land-locked Canadian province bordered by Alberta to the west and Manitoba to the east. To the south, Saskatchewan province forms the border between America's northern states of Montana and North Dakota. My parents, Arthur John and Martha Matley, were pioneers.

My father, known as Jack, was the youngest of eight children born to James and Lucy Matley on an estate called Bramshott in Hampshire, England. His father was coachman to Sir William Erle, a retired judge and politician, and his mother was a lady's maid in the same house. Sir William, who was fond of horses, dogs, and cattle, had no children of his own, and took an interest in the Matley clan. My two oldest uncles spent a lot of time with the local curate, a man named Leadbeater. He later became a famous spiritualist and was notorious for his relationships with young boys in America and Australia. I don't know how that affected them—Uncle Frank became a schoolteacher and Uncle Jim ended up in Papua—which greatly influenced my own life.

When my grandfather retired, the family moved to Guildford in Surrey, but a humdrum town life did not appeal to my father, who was still a teenager. He went to London, where he was apprenticed as a photoengraver in a printing works. In 1900, when he was nineteen years old, he joined the 2nd Kent Artillery Volunteers, earning a modest allowance for weekend drills and class training. Father became familiar with nine-pounder guns and siege howitzers on the practice ranges at Lydd, a small town in Kent, during annual summer camps, little thinking that he would one day put this knowledge into savage practice.

Jack met my mother, Martha Parfect, a few years later, and they married in September 1905 at St Saviour's church in Surrey. By then my father's parents were dead, and his siblings had scattered across England and abroad. Martha's widower father, a carpenter, was healthy and still living in the town of Reading, in county Berkshire. The newlyweds talked about starting a new life elsewhere and began researching opportunities for emigration. Their good friends, the Glovers, had already made the journey to Canada and were comfortably settled in a town in the province of Manitoba.

They learned that Canada had an emigration office in London and the country was advertising cheap land to people willing to travel to the prairies to build a homestead and set up as farmers.

While my parents loved the England they knew, with its soft green rolling hills, thatched cottages and ruined medieval abbeys, their reality had become the grittier drudge of city life in London. Canada lured them with catchy phrases:

An idyllic prairie life of blue skies, golden crops, happy families, friendly neighbours, sunshine and independence. The perfect place to raise a family. For six hundred Canadian dollars, anyone could buy 160 acres. The only condition placed on landholders was they must build a house and produce a crop for three years.

My parents signed up. Jack and Martha departed Liverpool on a warm spring day in April 1906, travelling second class on the *Lake Erie*, a four-masted, single-funnel ship.

Arthur (Jack) and Martha Matley, prior to emigration,
Croydon, England

From Montreal they travelled by train to Brandon, Manitoba to stay with the Glovers. Mother was five months pregnant when they sailed, and they were still boarding with the Glover family in Brandon when my eldest brother Francis was born that September.

At their first opportunity, Jack and Martha travelled by horse-drawn wagon to have their first view of their property. The land assigned to them was near a little prairie town called Punnichy, about sixtry-two miles north of Regina, the capital of Saskatchewan.

Instead of prosperous farms and settlements, they saw miles of rocky plains dotted with small lakes, patches of unfamiliar grass, and marshes. It was a wilderness that seemed unsuited for tilling and growing crops. Disappointment and disillusionment overwhelmed them.

While they stood staring around at the unpromising landscape, a man riding bareback on a horse approached. He wore a soft leather shirt, trousers, and moccasins. A rifle rested across the animal's neck, and hanging from his belt, two hares dripped blood. Father asked who he was and what he was doing on their land? The rider told him it was Saulteaux land, and according to treaty, the local tribes could use all the land for hunting. That was another shock for the Matleys—an English upbringing had not prepared them to deal with other cultures.

Jack and Martha had no idea of the contested history of the 160 acres they were to clear and settle. The first missionaries had appeared in the area in the 1820s, and white settlers began clearing land in the 1870s, displacing the traditional owners whose right to their lands was established in treaties signed at Fort Qu'Appelle in 1874. However, in 1882, when surveyors began dividing up the 160-acre blocks, the Métis (offspring of fur traders and native inhabitants), the Plains Indians, and the earlier white settlers were all apprehensive that they would lose their lands and accused the government of Ottawa of not respecting treaties.

In March 1885, a Métis leader and French Catholic named Louis Riel led the North-West Rebellion, an uprising against government forces. Defeated at the Battle of Batoche, Riel was hanged for high treason, and action that divided the country along French and English lines. Twenty years later, when the Matleys took up their claim, the linguistic, religious and racial differences were far from resolved. Four groups of Plains Indians were living on reserves in the Touchwood Hills surrounding Punnichy. The treaties signed in 1874 had established the tribes' rights to the reserves, and they weren't going anywhere.

Father bought two cows and paid to have a twelve by twenty-foot log cabin built. When this was completed in September 1907, he immediately started work on a larger building. Spruce logs, debarked and dried, were notched and stacked onto a wooden floor. Roof rafters were then laid onto the stacked logs, an iron roof was placed on the rafters and the windows cut out.

Mother and Father worked long hours to clear their land of rocks, all done by hand. Thousands of rocks had to be removed with a crowbar and pick and placed in piles before the land could be ploughed. Memories of the soft green hills, village life, relatives, and close neighbours now seemed like a dream. She thought her daily chores pleasant compared with the rock clearing.

Martha holding baby Francis, Brandon, Manitoba, 1906

James (Jim) Matley on a visit to Canada, 1907

In 1907, Father broke four and a half acres for barley and oats, walking behind a steel plough attached to a team of horses. A crew who moved from farm to farm harvested the crops and delivered them to the grain elevators next to the railway line. Father signed a statutory declaration in March 1908 stating he had complied with all the government requirements. He had built and lived in the residence and intended to crop and fence the acres he had already worked and comply with the law each year until he was entitled to have his patent issued. That year, eleven more acres were ploughed and four and a half cropped. In 1909 my sister, Mary, was born. Father sowed another fifteen acres of crop. In 1910 he bought another eight cows, and successfully applied to have his homestead patent issued, proving he had met all the Canadian government's settlement requirements.

While breaking the ground, Father sometimes flushed out prairie chickens (a type of grouse) or rabbits which he brought home to supplement our meals. As well as the ready supply of meat, my mother had a thriving vegetable garden which kept the family fed. Vegetables included corn, capsicums, peas, cucumbers, beans and carrots. She preserved what was left over, either by drying or cooking the vegetables in jars. She also had milk from the cows and made her own butter and cream, which she took two miles into town, in a horse and gig, to exchange for flour and sugar. Of course, she made her own bread. Laundry took two days or more to complete, and then there was ironing and mending, as well as preparing and cooking food.

Despite the hard work, the small acreage meant the crops did not produce an adequate income. Father found outside work as a teamster, hauling goods on a wagon with a team of horses. The flood of immigrants to the area after 1900 had led to an expansion of the Canadian Northern Railway, which built new lines to Regina, Saskatoon, Prince Albert, and Edmonton, and pushed on through the Yellowhead Pass. Men laid sleepers, built trestle bridges, and cut and filled the line of track. Father was busy with contracts to haul materials and supplies and this took him away from home for long periods.

Mother took over the day-to-day running of the farm. One day she was sitting outside the homestead. It was blisteringly hot, and the house was like an oven. She set up her treasured pink umbrella to shelter her from the burning sun. What a contrast, she thought, to the constant soft rains of England she had often complained about but now longed for. A local indigenous youth wandering over the farm tried to take the bright umbrella from her. As they both struggled for it, she screamed. The youth fled in fright. She was frightened, too. Sobbing and gasping for breath, she gathered the children, and the umbrella, retreated into that stifling house and bolted the door. In her imagination, she feared the family could be scalped, murdered, and the house burned down.

She hated living out there, on that desolate farm. The nights spent on her own were the worst. After the children were asleep in their bed, she would step outside and scream across the paddocks, into the prairie wind where the sound was scooped up and carried off into the darkness. Across the vast prairie, outside a thousand log cabins, she imagined other women were doing the same.

Nearly a year after Mother had her third child, Arthur, in December 1912, she received word that her father was unwell and not expected to survive. Father made arrangements for the family to travel back to England. My grandfather held on until Christmas Day 1913, then died the next day. I was born in February 1914 and christened in St John's church in Reading. We stayed in England with relatives until the end of July and were at sea on the *Empress of Britain* when war broke out on 4 August 1914.

Back in Punnichy, Father was anxious to join the war effort. After nearly a year away, the farm no longer held his attention, and Mother was keen to move into town. Like other countries of the British Empire, it took a while for the Canadian government to mobilise its forces. In early 1915, Father joined the 5th Brigade which formed part of the 2nd Canadian Division of the Canadian Expeditionary Force. After he left, Mother and the children stayed in a boarding house in Calgary before moving back to their familiar surroundings in Punnichy.

Father never spoke to me about his war experience. I know he arrived in England for training in August 1915, then went to France at the beginning of 1916. His background in the Artillery Volunteers led to a position in a gun battery where he was promoted to corporal and then sergeant. He served in France and Flanders until the end of the war, and probably fought with the Canadians at places like the Somme, Arras, Cambrai and so on, until the final assaults on the Hindenburg line. I'm pretty sure he was at Vimy Ridge, where many Canadians fought. He wrote the following letter to a comrade's family, who had it published in the local paper:

Last year while things were very warm around the battery, four of us on the gun crew took each other's home addresses and arranged if anything happened to write home and let those most interested know.

I am the only one left of the four, so it is up to me to keep my promise to 'Liz,' as we always called him, to write to you. There is really very little to say. We are again in a warm corner and a shell burst close to 'Liz,' killing him instantly and the army lost a first-class soldier, and we lost a staunch comrade. His body was brought back that night and is now buried behind the line in company with hosts of other brave lads who have laid down their lives in the fight for freedom and justice.

In closing, I should like to express my very deep sympathy with you in your great loss and to tell you how much we all felt the loss of your son who was so popular with us all.

About six weeks before the war was to end, Father was helping to unload an 18-pounder gun from a motor lorry. As the gun ran out it struck a shell hole causing the trail, the heavy iron arms on the carriage, to swing sharply to the right. The ground was soft. Father slipped trying to get out of the way and the trail fell on his foot. He was evacuated to England where he spent three months in hospital before being sent home to Canada. In that hospital, A. A. Beattie, another gunner from the 20th Battery, wrote this little poem:

A happy family are we,
With nothing to do but drink our tea.
If we like reading there's books galore,
Or if we like noise,
Play the piano some more,
Or if our brain gets active
And needs something to do
Then there are puzzles and games for ten, one or two.
It's now 8 o'clock
And no more I can tell
As the nurse at the door
Is ringing the bell.

Mother had never expected a world war would improve her life, but it did. It allowed her, along with her four children, to live in town where she made friends and survived on part of a soldier's wage and family allowance. I have very few memories of that time, as I was quite small. However, I remember the day Father was due to return. Mother sent us to greet him at the station on our own. Francis was thirteen, Mary ten, Arthur seven, and I was five. I never knew why she did not go with us.

There were many people crowded on the platform, but we managed to squeeze through to the front. The engine was idling with a rhythmic panting when the carriage doors opened, releasing its passengers. A strange man in uniform appeared before us, walking with a limp. Francis and Mary recognised Father and were soon hugging him, but Arthur and I hung back. I didn't know who he was! Then this uniformed man disentangled himself and held out his arms to us.

Big Hill and the surrounding Touchwood Hills distinguished Punnichy from most other prairie towns, which were mainly built on flat prairie land.

Our small house was on a road that led towards Big Hill from which you could get a panoramic view of the surrounding countryside. It was also a favourite playground of the town's children, mainly in winter when we'd slide down its snow-covered western slope on sleds.

The seasons were memorable for their extremes in temperature. In summer the poplars were golden yellow and the pin cherry bushes were a flaming crimson. Depending on the season, swimming, horseback riding, ice hockey, skiing, or ice skating filled our leisure time.

But the winters were punishing. Wind chills often brought temperatures below minus twenty degrees Fahrenheit. Snow would be banked high against the window, and my bedside glass of water would usually freeze. In the morning I'd grit my teeth and throw back the heavy blankets and warm eiderdown which had cocooned me during the night. Over my cotton flannel pyjamas, I'd pull on thick woollen trousers, a heavy cotton shirt, a fur coat and hat, and plod down the stairs to the kitchen. Before venturing outside, I'd step into stiff, cold, fur-lined boots, pull on thick woollen mittens and wrap a woollen scarf around my face. My lungs would burn as I breathed in the freezing air. Thick, powdery snow covered the woodpile. I'd clumsily brush the snow off, load a basket with kindling and logs and carry them inside. The kitchen fire had usually died down to embers during the night and needed rekindling. As it burned, the iciness of the room would slowly slip away.

Francis, Culver, Arthur (jnr.), Martha and Mary Matley, 1914

Father became the town's postmaster, so we lived above and behind the post office. My parents were also responsible for the central switchboard of the telephone exchange, and they got to know everyone's business. Punnichy, at that time, was a small village, with wooden sidewalks and dirt roads. There was no piped water supply or sewerage system, but several water pumps around the town provided us with water. When they froze in winter, Arthur and I had to gather snow to melt for washing and drinking.

Outside of their post office work, Mother and Father both made substantial contributions to the life of the village. Father served as Union Sunday School's superintendent, councillor, and overseer. He also joined the Touchwood Great War Veterans Association, and Mother joined the Ladies Auxiliary of the Royal Canadian Legion.

Our little school, a timber framed building around thirty-six feet by twenty-four feet, had been built in 1909 and became overcrowded after the war. In 1920 there were fifty-five pupils in grades one to three, and twenty-two in grades four to nine. A new four-roomed two-story brick school was opened in 1923, when I was nine. Students from the four Indian Reserves surrounding Punnichy also attended the school, and indeed, several indigenous families lived in the village. Many of their children were my school friends and playmates. They were good students and fine athletes.

As young adults we travelled by train to Saskatoon for our tertiary education and boarded with church families. It was a small rural city about 143 miles away, serving the surrounding agricultural district. Francis, the eldest, was the first to leave home. He achieved high marks in a civil service examination and later served as a librarian in the Library of the Canadian Parliament in Ottawa. My sister Mary became a teacher and worked and taught in the local area. Arthur left school at sixteen to take a business course in Saskatoon and later found work there as an accountant.

I was always interested in engines and how things worked, and I was good with my hands. I was fascinated by the special silk trains hauling Japanese silk from the Pacific Coast ports to the eastern textile mills. They roared through Punnichy, shaking the whole town, while the shriek of their steam whistles reverberated over the hills. Armed guards riding shotgun on million-dollar shipments added to the thrill. The peak year was 1929, when over 500,000 bales, or more than $325 million worth of raw silk, were transported on the railway.

The main reason for the race across the continent was fluctuations in the price of raw silk. Interest on money tied up

Culver, Mary, Francis, Martha, Arthur jnr., 1930s

in a large shipment was appreciable, and insurance on the goods in transit was exceptionally high. A delay of even a few hours could cost importers thousands of dollars. Another reason was the danger of banditry. The silk trains ended in the mid-1930s with the increase in man-made fibres and the easier passage of the Panama Canal.

I decided to study mechanical engineering. Before I left home to begin my first year of study, my Uncle Jim visited, and I warmed to him immediately. A tall man, with a walrus moustache and a commanding presence, he had me captivated with his stories of a far-off land: the tropics of Papua New Guinea. His descriptions of its people, the climate, and his financial success managing a copra plantation made me envious.

Uncle Jim had established plantations in Queensland in 1912, but was now running Waigani, a plantation in Papua owned by the Lever Brothers. To get to Waigani you first had to sail to a little island called Samarai, the administrative and business centre, and Papua's main port. He showed me where it was on a map, in the China Strait, just off the coast of southeast Papua New Guinea. Waigani plantation was a few hours by petrol boat from the mainland. As Uncle Jim spoke, my dissatisfaction with the country I grew up in mounted. He brought a vision of another life, unimaginable and unattainable to me. Or so I thought at the time.

Saskatchewan experienced its first drought in 1929 and had undergone three crop failures by 1931. Rain returned in 1932 producing good crops, but low prices gave the farmers poor returns. Rain fell again in the spring of 1933, and though the crop started well, a plague of grasshoppers destroyed it.

During 1934, in my second year of study, the winds of change were gathering. Temperatures soared, the wind blew, and local fairs were cancelled because no one had any produce to exhibit. I witnessed the heartbreaking sight of the once lush prairie fields and wheat crops withering under the unrelenting sun, described well by Bruce Dyck in *The Western Producer*:

> *Hot drying winds scooped up loose topsoil into dust blizzards that made outside activity nearly impossible.*
>
> *An estimated quarter of a million acres of Saskatchewan land was blowing out of control by the mid-1930s.*
>
> *Darkness at noon was not uncommon, while churning dirt piled up in drifts along buildings, fence lines or ridges ... until another wind comes up to move it somewhere else.*

We put wet rags and sheets under doorways and over windowsills to keep the dust out. It drifted in any way, coating everything with a thick film. With the relentless heat and wind, and the lack of water, home gardens died, and any that struggled on usually succumbed to the plagues of green army worms and grasshoppers that stripped anything that was left.

The fertile prairies once referred to as 'The Bread Bowl' were now a dust bowl. The Saskatchewan government was borrowing heavily, spending more on relief than its total revenues. Photographs of drifting sand and the bleached bones of Saskatchewan cows appeared in newspapers all over Canada. Folk from the more fortunate parts of the country responded to the disaster with truckloads of fruit, fish, vegetables and canned foods sent to needy districts.

People left in droves, abandoning their farms. I only had another year to complete my engineering course, but there was no money to pay for my board and fees. Fortunately, my father still had his post office job, but he couldn't afford to support me through another year of study. My only option was to look for work in Saskatoon, but I had little hope of finding some there.

I wrote to my Uncle Jim in Papua New Guinea outlining my difficulties and asked if he could find some work for me on his plantation. I waited anxiously each day for a reply.

Tepees, Punnichy, 1930s

My New Life Begins: Samarai Island and Papua 1935

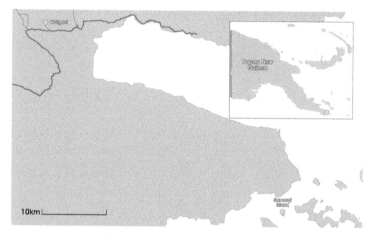

Samarai, Papua New Guinea

Samarai jetty, ca. 1927

I had never been a great reader, more of a sporting type, but in those weeks I worked my way through Ballantyne's *The Coral Island*, Defoe's *Robinson Crusoe*, and a good few more just to get an idea of what it might be like to live on a tropical island. I dreamed of palm trees, white sand, and no snow.

At last, a letter arrived from Uncle Jim offering me a temporary job 'while I found my feet'. If I accepted, he would telegraph money for a one-way passage as an advance on my wages. My parents were reluctant to let their youngest child travel so far away, and we had some lively discussions about it. I argued that they had lived in England, and Father had seen France, and I wanted to see the world too. We discussed the benefits, and more importantly, what I was leaving behind. Was I ready to leave my home, family, friends, and the only way of life I knew?

I was twenty-one, old enough to make up my own mind, and I had little chance of getting a proper job in Canada. Knowing I would be in reliable hands with Uncle Jim, my parents finally gave their blessing. The thought of leaving everything behind, with no idea if I would ever be able to return, did weigh heavily on me. But I was young and eager to try something completely different, perhaps even dangerous, and that idea thrilled me.

There was a whirl of activity as I settled my limited affairs and said goodbye to my many friends. Then, one Friday evening in early September 1935, about forty friends gathered in the Punnichy Community Hall for a proper farewell. There was singing, instrumental music, and more speeches than I really cared for. There had been a whip-around, and I was given a purse of money, for which I was very grateful. A report of the affair even made it into a Saskatoon newspaper.

I travelled halfway across Canada by train to Vancouver, expecting to join the MV *Aorangi*, a combination of ocean liner and refrigerated cargo ship. It was named after a mountain on the South Island of New Zealand and had been the world's largest and fastest motor ship when it was launched ten years earlier. However, I was disappointed to learn that the *Aorangi* was being refitted in Sydney, and I would be travelling on the slower SS *Monowai*.

We departed on 9 October, and I soon warmed to the *Monowai*. Named after a lake in New Zealand, her hull was painted bronze-green, she had a white superstructure, and her funnels were red with black caps. Each of her reciprocating engines had an exhaust turbine, with a total output of nearly 15,000 horsepower, giving a maximum speed of nineteen knots. You can bet I found a way to visit the engine room. I was fascinated by the whole noisy setup and went back several times, and got to know one of the engineering officers.

We stopped at Honolulu, Suva and Auckland, and arrived in Sydney on Saturday 2 November, with 250 passengers onboard. Some were anxious to get on to Melbourne for the Cup on the following Tuesday, talking about a favourite called Peter Pan. I spent more than a week in Sydney, exploring on foot and by tram its streets and hills, the beautiful harbour reminded me in some ways of Vancouver's harbour, though my experience of harbours was very limited at that time. The huge arch of the Sydney Harbour Bridge, which was just three years old, was amazing. A bright new amusement park, called Luna Park, had opened a month earlier at Milsons Point, the site where the workshops had been for the bridge construction. I went across by ferry and entered through the clown's mouth, meeting some other young people for a day of fun.

I was booked on the Burns Philp passenger and cargo ship, SS *Montoro* and made a point of watching her come into Walsh Bay from Rabaul on the following Wednesday. As I stood on the wharf looking at the smoke drifting from *Montoro's* single funnel, I promised myself I would return to this beautiful city. After a few days unloading and loading, she was ready to depart. The *Montoro* carried all sorts of goods including tinned fish, meat, rice, flour, sugar, tobacco, mail, and beer and spirits.

We called in at Brisbane, Townsville, Cairns and Port Moresby before arriving at Samarai, so I had a gradual introduction to the tropics. As we travelled north, the days grew warmer with a fresh sea breeze tempering the heat. We were fortunate, according to the captain, that we didn't experience any of the tropical storms that regularly occurred in this part of the world. The cabins became unbearably hot, so the ship's deck was the preferred place to be and the best place to view the spectacular sunsets and clear, starry nights. We were given a choice of eating our meals on deck or in the state rooms. There was a choice of soup, fish, grills, or cold meat with salad. Sweets included golden rolls with syrup, coconut custard and London buns. There was no maple syrup, so I acclimatised with the coconut custard.

I didn't pay much attention to Port Moresby, thinking it second-rate compared to the Australian ports, not realising how important it would be to me in the future.

On the morning we were to sail into Samarai port, the ship passed many small coral islands fringed with coconut palms. I saw scenes I'd only read about in books and in the newspaper clippings Uncle Jim had posted to me. I thought of places evoked by those newspapers: the '… *coral lagoons with all the glorious colouring of scintillating opals set in white filigree of foamy reefs, multi-coloured fish, like butterflies, flitting among the coral flowers visible in the clear sea water.*'

A tropical fairyland of bright sunshine, white sand, white houses with red roofs, and green tops of coconut trees appeared as we neared the island. I closed my eyes for a second and inhaled the hothouse air which carried the scent of spices mixed with the fragrance of flowering tropical trees I couldn't yet name.

The ship's arrival brought nearly all the town's inhabitants down to the wharf. Laughing, brown-skinned boys decked in flowers paddled their canoes alongside the ship. Loud laughter and chatter came from the wharf, and on opening my eyes I saw dozens of brown-skinned men with thick frizzy hair waiting for our ship to dock and unload its cargo. Bare-chested and wearing brightly coloured loincloths, they sat, squatted, and stood in happy groups, chattering in their language.

Samarai Island was very tiny, only fifty-four acres and one could walk around it in twenty minutes, and the houses, with their large verandahs, were generously spaced out. There were three warves, a large one for steamers and two narrow ones for smaller craft. On the big wharf, open grass-thatched barns stored goods for export such as copra, packages of rubber, trochus shell and *bêche-de-mer*.

Though small in size, Samarai was an important trading centre for the mainland of Papua New Guinea and the many islands clustered around its south-eastern extremity. All the trade from marine, coconut, rubber and mining products went through this port.

A small group of European men dressed in white suits stood apart from the crowd, and I spotted my uncle among them. He stood out, his tall, slim figure with white Panama atop, hands in pockets, his unmistakable bushy moustache and an elegantly carved pipe between his lips.

I leapt off the gangplank and greeted my uncle enthusiastically. As we chatted and caught up with each other's news, he showed me around the town which looked and felt as I had imagined. Nothing disappointed me.

The indigenous men, women, and children were all almost naked, and I couldn't help staring. The women wore beautiful grass skirts which swayed as they walked.

Samarai

Noticing my interest, Uncle Jim promptly said that if I pursued any Papuan women I would be ostracised from white society. Also, I couldn't raise my hand to strike any person, or the law would take care of me with a fine, or possibly jail.

I didn't need telling twice.

James (Jim) Matley

There were no vehicles and no roads, just a pleasant wide path of crushed coral going around the island from which the paths branched off to the various houses. There were three hotels, a bakery, an engineering workshop, the Burns Philp and Steamships Company stores, a church and a hospital. There was also a cricket ground, tennis courts, and best of all, a pool built right on the beach which was regularly flushed by the ocean currents sweeping through the China Strait.

I looked at that sparkling pool and thought the contrast with Punnichy and Saskatchewan couldn't have been starker. It was probably minus twenty on another wind-blasted winter's day at home. I squinted at my white shirt, trying to imagine it as snow. Nope, no way I wanted to be back there.

Samarai was a place for shopping, entertainment and repairing the equipment used on the mainland plantations. We spent the rest of the day shopping for supplies and stayed the night in a hotel before boarding a boat for the thirty-mile trip north to the Papuan coast, then a fifteen-mile truck journey inland to Waigani.

I soon learned that managers, including my uncle, had to build their own roads and be self-sufficient in many ways. Food was grown on the plantations and wood was harvested from the forest. My uncle traded in copra and managed plantations on other islands and the mainland. Copra, the dried meat of coconuts, was an essential ingredient for soap, as well as being a food source. Lever Brothers, who owned the plantation, were soap manufacturers.

It was also my first experience with houseboys, a common term for the young men who worked as servants. It took me some time to get used to people waiting on me. They were paid, had housing and food provided, and wore white calico skirts, or ramis, which covered the body from the waist down to the calves. The tops of their bodies were bare. I found them very superstitious, a result I'm guessing, of little or no contact with the outside world. If they became sick they would turn their faces to the wall and prepare to die, because they thought it was the will of the 'spirit man'.

I worked and lived in the main house on the Waigani plantation, which allowed me to try out various jobs around the copra-drying sheds and the palm plantations, and learn the basics of Motu, the local language. Most of my work involved fixing small engines and machinery.

Uncle Jim and his wife, my aunt Elspeth, had a son Charles who was away boarding at Geelong Grammar. Sadly, another son, Guy, had died at Kings School in Sydney four years earlier. Because of their remoteness, they didn't hear about his illness and burial until after the funeral. I think they were pleased to have another young Matley around the plantation.

Occasionally, Uncle Jim sent me to relieve a manager on a neighbouring property. The reasons varied, but mostly the permanent manager was going on leave, and they preferred a white manager as a replacement, never mind the lack of experience, just someone capable. The managerial role was a steep learning curve, but I was fortunate to have competent boss boys (native foremen). They did most of the work in selecting work gangs and supervising the workforce while I provided occasional guidance.

I also helped supervise the weeding of newly planted trees, which was the most intensive task and necessary to enable the young palms to grow. The locals had found ingenious ways to deal with the weeds. By planting wild passionfruit, maize, sweet potato and cowpeas, they blanketed the weeds, which killed them, and provided a substantial amount of food as well. The undergrowth, thick and lush, housed thousands of snakes. On one occasion, a python slithered into the chook house through a hole in the fence. It was trapped as it was too swollen to get out again. One of the workers caught it and cut it open. The snake had swallowed two chooks and a duck.

After six months, and over a whiskey on the veranda, Uncle Jim laid out his plans for me. He mentioned that George Loudon was looking for a junior assistant. I had met Mr Loudon on one of his visits to Waigani and was impressed, as was anyone who met him. His unofficial title was the King of Papua.

Mr Loudon had plans to expand his plantations, Mororo and Eilogo on the Sogeri Plateau in the hills behind Port Moresby. Uncle Jim said he had recommended me because I had the skills needed, was capable, with a sense of adventure and had a willingness to work hard. Needless to say, in those days, only a young white male would do.

I knew I would be sorry to leave Waigani and my extended family, but it seemed an opportunity not to be missed. There was no shortage of vessels travelling from Samarai to Port Moresby, but the weather was bad, and I was a bit apprehensive. Samarai had experienced fourteen inches of rain in late June and the cricket pitch was under water. A ketch returning from a recruiting trip capsized, drowning nine labourers. Still, I went ahead, showing Uncle Jim that my sense of adventure was still intact.

Pre-War:
Mororo and Eilogo
1936

Rouna Falls

As I sailed into Port Moresby harbour, I was disappointed with the sight of the town. It looked dry and dusty, even with the hills and mountains in the background. The lush vegetation and colour I had become used to at Waigani and Samarai were absent. Iron-roofed, timber-framed houses scattered the hills and the coconut palms fringing the harbour provided the only relief from the drab landscape.

Mr Loudon, smartly dressed in the typical settler style of white jodhpurs, matching short-sleeved shirt with breast pockets, tie and a white Panama hat, was waiting to meet me. He shook my hand warmly and when I told him of my disappointment with the town, he explained they had not had much rain and people were buying water and saying the climate had changed. It was the dry season, and he assured me that where we were going—up to the Sogeri Plateau in the mountains—the climate would be much cooler and wetter.

We travelled thirty miles on a narrow, red-dirt road in a truck carrying bags of rice, flour and sugar for the plantations. These goods were a back-loading for the baled and cured rubber brought down. Once we'd left Moresby and reached the foothills of the mountains, I forgot all about my initial disappointment in the landscape.

The road followed the Laloki River, which corkscrewed around the foothills of the Astrolabe Range. As we climbed and the temperature dropped, the thundering of water became louder and louder. A carpet of vibrant green draped the valleys. Beside the road lay massive ink-coloured volcanic boulders scattered like giant, misshapen bowling balls. The dark clouds dropped lower, and the lightning increased, closely followed by ear-splitting thunder.

As we reached a staging post, a small hotel at Rouna Falls, dark, rain-filled clouds had moved lower, obscuring the higher peaks. Lightning flickered and warning rumbles sounded through the valley. The view from the hotel took full advantage of the falls plunging three hundred feet into the Laloki River gorge below. No matter how many times I travelled that road in the years after, I never tired of seeing it.

A line of mules, hitched nose to tail, was assembled on the muddy ground in front of the hotel. While we drank tea and ate lunch, plantation hands transferred the truck's goods onto the waiting mules. We would travel the last few miles on foot.

A steep track ran eastward from the hotel, climbing for half a mile until it reached the river above the falls. Here a ford crossed the river, which became impossible to cross after heavy rain. We led the mules across to where the track divided, at the edge of the Sogeri Plateau. Mr Loudon told me that the track diverging to the north led to Kokoda village. The mule train continued east and in about a mile reached the edge of the sprawling village of Sogeri. The mule handlers divided up the pack animals, and some left with their loads for the town or plantations further east.

I stayed with the main group which travelled south-east following the river's eastern bank. The track continued, winding along the slopes of moderate hills and keeping above the dense vegetation of the valley floor. After about a mile we turned left up a short hill toward Mororo, but we didn't stop. Mr Loudon said we would return in the morning when he'd show me my accommodation and go over in more detail, my duties and the operational side of things.

We continued along a steadily descending track, and the vegetation grew denser as we neared the edge of the clearings and plantations of Eilogo, about a mile and a half beyond Mororo. We arrived at dusk, exhausted from our travels, and the heavens opened again with thunder and rain. The plantation hands managed to unload everything at the trade store before quickly heading to their accommodation and safety. We sheltered under the porch of the trade store, watching the storm in all its glorious fury.

Between the volleys of simultaneous lightning strikes and roaring thunder, Mr Loudon quickly sketched out the work he expected me to do. It was some years before he would allow me to call him George, and his wife, Peg. Until then it was Mr and Mrs Loudon. My work would mainly be maintaining the plant's equipment and supervising the labourers working on his coffee and rubber holdings.

Mr and Mrs Loudon lived in a house set on a knoll and built around an enormous central garden of ornamental shrubs and ferns. Mr Loudon had engaged an architect from Sydney, who specialised in tropical houses, to design it. The building was cool and spacious. Polished concrete floors ran beside the rectangular garden, and teak beams held up the open roof. The kitchen, bedrooms and living areas faced the garden.

I was very impressed. I came to live there many years later, but that's a story for another time. The entire one thousand acre property was self-contained. A home garden provided European vegetables, a bakery turned out 240 loaves of bread a day, and pies and biscuits for the labour force. There was a well-stocked trade store, a sawmill and a petrol station.

The following morning Mr Loudon showed me my accommodation at Mororo. My house was simple and well-built on wooden stilts, designed to keep the house cool. Bamboo, split, plaited and lashed with vines and string made the walls, and the roof was thatched grass.

I quickly settled into the same work routine I was familiar with from my time at Waigani—maintaining machinery, training drivers, training tappers and organising various work groups. If I had any energy left at the end of the day, I'd read or listen to my short-wave wireless set. Weekends were a diversion from the daily work schedule. There was an excellent social network between neighbouring plantations, and I often received lunch or dinner invitations. At other times I'd hike through the plantation or forests, getting to know the country, and I enjoyed swimming in the mountain streams.

Our days started with a coffee and smoke at 5:30 am. At 6:00 am, the boss boy would ring a bell to summon the labourers, who, after having their breakfast, would turn up ready for work. I handed out lunches and Mr Loudon would check if anyone had any sores or was sick. Mr Loudon was allowed to administer drugs and to give injections and would allocate jobs to those who could work, while he treated the people needing medical attention. I watched and learned. Besides cut feet, the major illnesses included colds, dysentery, malaria, yaws and tropical ulcers. Yaws, a tropical skin infection, showed up as lesions on the face, hands and feet.

To do this medical work, Mr Loudon had qualified and received a medical certificate in tropical diseases from Port Moresby Hospital. Later, I did the same. The course also

Rubber tapping

Rubber drying

covered the practical side of injections, penicillin, morphine, snake bites, stitching up wounds. It was a legal requirement for all those who employed indigenous labour, especially in isolated locations. At one of these roll calls I asked Mr Loudon if he ever had to discipline anyone, to which he quickly replied that he had the law on his side. If anyone refused to work, they were sacked and if they threatened him, it was court and jail. There was no need to be a bully.

Before I arrived, Mr Loudon, to spread his investment risks, had interplanted his rubber trees with two varieties of coffee. He had been disillusioned with the fluctuating rubber price and planned to convert Eilogo entirely to coffee. Buyers in Sydney were impressed by its quality and Mr Loudon initially found a ready market. However, over-production in Brazil and elsewhere caused the coffee market to slump, and Mr Loudon couldn't compete. He appealed to Australia for support without success.

An inefficient transport system for carrying stores, supplies, and coffee was a significant problem. The rubber and coffee crops were transported from the plantations to Rouna by mule, then the goods went by truck to Port Moresby, and then onto the ships, with supplies coming to the plantations in the reverse order. When I arrived, the price of coffee had fallen so low that Mr Loudon decided the crop wasn't worth harvesting. With the coffee plants in full flower, I was given the disheartening duty of helping pull them all out. All that work and promise ended up on a bonfire. The rubber price was rising, and the only hope to improve returns was to plant more trees.

After the coffee debacle, reducing costs became a priority,

with mule and truck freight high on the list. Mr Loudon brought advisers to Eilogo who selected an area on the eastern side of the plantation to be cleared for an aerodrome. Clearing the jungle was no easy task, and we had to do it all by hand with axes and machetes. By June 1938, enough area was cleared to land a Guinea Airways tri-motored Ford plane. On its first two flights from Port Moresby it carried three thousand lbs of cargo in each load. With one passenger, each trip took only sixty minutes barring any unforeseen incidents. Previously, that shipment would have required six motor trucks and drivers, thirty mules with local attendants, and at least one week to have goods delivered to or from Eilogo.

The air freight service became reasonably regular, though always subject to the vagaries of the weather. Mr Loudon's seventeen-year-old son Ian, home at Christmas from his school in Australia, was fascinated by the aircraft and was determined to learn to fly. There was no opportunity at the plantation, but Ian was to get his chance in a way we could not have expected.

The year 1939 was a momentous one for me. First, in May, I received the shocking news of my Uncle James's death. He and his wife, Elspeth, had been visiting her brother in Melbourne when he suddenly died from a heart attack. We had kept in constant contact since Samarai and had visited each other several times. His death was a deep loss for me. It made me realise just how far I was from my parents, and how little chance there was of seeing them any time soon.

Then, more bad news. Reports from abroad started sounding ominous. Japan had already taken over Manchuria in the early 1930s and was expanding further into China, with plans to dominate the Asia-Pacific region. Our everyday life was untouched, but I knew that world events and politics had a way of interfering, even here. The village drums, once a sign of celebration, now sent out a beat of unease and disquiet. Then came the worst news. On 1 September 1939, the headlines announced that the Nazis had invaded Poland, and only two days later, that Britain and France had declared war on Germany. Australia and Canada were part of the British Empire, and therefore, according to the Australian Prime Minister Robert Menzies, we were automatically at war, too.

Clearing land for rubber plantation

41

War Years:
Middle East
1941

68 Light Aid Detachment.
Culver back row, fourth from left

In mid-May 1940, I heard on the evening news that the Nazis had invaded Luxembourg, the Netherlands and Belgium. The Luftwaffe bombings left some cities unrecognisable. German paratroopers were dropped into the Netherlands and seized control of critical bridges and other infrastructure. The Germans then moved into France, and Paris fell in mid-June. The news was incomplete, but I made sure the radio was warmed up by six o'clock every evening.

We knew the Japanese had been fighting in Manchuria and China, but when they invaded Vietnam, Laos and Cambodia in September 1940, they were entering PNG's backyard. It seemed the Western defences were crumbling. Along with countless others, I thought our British heritage and way of life was under threat. I decided my PNG home was worth fighting for.

I wanted to enlist in the army, but I couldn't do it in Port Moresby. Reinforcements were being recruited for the 2nd Australian Imperial Force (AIF), which was the volunteer force designated to serve overseas, but there were quotas for each state and none for PNG. In accordance with the mandate of the League of Nations, there were no fortifications, and no naval or military bases in PNG. There was a lot of local concern about able-bodied men heading south to enlist, and some plantations had been left in the charge of women, which was unacceptable to many at the time.

I had a lot to think about, and it wasn't practicable to travel back to Canada to enlist. Anyway, my birth certificate stated that I was born in Reading, England. In the end, I travelled to Sydney where I found the army was reporting a calamitous shortage of artisans and tradesmen. Nearly a thousand men were needed in New South Wales alone to complete existing units for overseas service, and men up to forty-five years old would be accepted for the Australian Army Field Workshops if physically fit. I was only twenty-six, very fit, and eager to start.

I found a recruitment centre at Victoria Barracks in Paddington, where I enlisted at the beginning of December 1940. They made me a private with the 3rd Division Army Field Workshops. I was well qualified for this role as I already knew about vehicles and machinery and could fix just about anything —brakes, wheel bearings, springs, radiator fittings, fuel lines and pumps, and simple electrical faults. Generally, I expected my responsibility would be to maintain machinery and keep it in good mechanical condition.

When we sailed from Sydney on 27 December 1940, it wasn't on one of those grand converted passenger liners like the *Queen Mary* and the *Queen Elizabeth*, with their relative comfort, but on the troopship *Glenpark*. This was a converted tramp ship, humble, inelegant and slow. We travelled with our equipment: Bren gun carriers, four-wheel drive trucks, mobile workshops and Jeeps. At the rear of the ship were two wooden structures, the cookhouse with its stoves and cooking gear, on the portside, and directly opposite on the starboard side, the toilet block with a metal trough, to which was attached a wooden bench with ten circular holes.

We swung out at full tide, escorted by launches and ferries carrying relatives and friends who waved and shouted their goodbyes, some playing hide-and-seek with the police launches, until the swell through the Heads turned them back. For the largely uneventful three-week journey, we were fully occupied with constant training. There were lifeboat drills, lectures, route marches around the boat decks, all kinds of physical training and deck sports. I guess they thought if they kept us busy, we would not misbehave!

As we sailed further north, the Southern Cross sank lower in the sky each night. It was a comfort and reminder of my adopted home until, after we passed through the Red Sea, it slipped from view. As the ship entered Port Tewfik, the gateway to the Suez Canal, the view of the mountains became clearer and the land looked sandy and barren. It was about here, I think, that Moses led the Israelites from Egypt to the promised land.

When we finally arrived at Tewfik, everyone was fed up with the never-ending exercises, lectures, and training—we were impatient to get back on land. But we had to sit through more lectures on how to behave towards the people of the Middle East before disembarkation could begin. After spending some time ashore to stretch our legs, Arab crews manning large open barges came alongside and ferried troops and equipment to a waiting troopship moored nearby. Tugs shouldered the barges from ship to ship.

At the beginning of February, in hot, uncomfortable weather, we travelled up the Suez Canal for most of a day, before disembarking at El Kantara. The city sprawled across both sides of the canal, around a hundred miles north-east of Egypt's capital city, Cairo. During the First World War, El Kantara had been a strategic defence post because of the Suez Canal, which runs almost directly north to Port Said where it joins the Mediterranean Sea. El Kantara was also a hospital and distribution centre during that time, and those centres had now been re-established. We enjoyed an excellent hot meal at a British staging camp, and with all the preparations and loading completed by dusk, we boarded a train to Palestine and our first camp. The Arab driver enjoyed tooting the whistle, loudly and often, during that night journey.

Culver in uniform, 1942

This first Middle East camp's main aim was to acclimatise newly arrived troops for three weeks. It was a wasteland of sand and sandhills. Not a skerrick of vegetation grew there. At breakfast I thought I'd try the local option of poached eggs in tomato sauce, swimming in a strange concoction of oil, onion and garlic. I took a sniff and after a quick taste, decided this wasn't for me and promptly reached for the army ration instead.

Endless route marches through sand, dust and heat are particularly memorable, as was the soreness of my muscles from constantly running up and down sandhills, practising bayonet charges. It was really a waste of time for the mechanics, apart from keeping us occupied, but perhaps a day would come when we needed that experience. Occasionally, there'd be spasmodic shots by the sentries at lurking Arabs or shadows.

The sand housed millions of fleas and often their bites festered requiring treatment. Dysentery became rife, too, and I'd see blokes vomiting and suffering diarrhoea simultaneously, but fortunately I didn't get it. Arab children hung around the camp selling the most delicious grapefruit and oranges which we traded for army biscuits or tinned food. Outside the camp some Arabs set up makeshift canvas stalls selling whatever they could, from liquor and tobacco to cameras and clothing. Picture nights were a welcome relief from the training. One I enjoyed was *The Man Who Wouldn't Talk*, a crime fiction sort of picture. Seating was either on trestles or the sand, as we watched the film under a sea of stars.

Once everyone had reached peak physical fitness, through the help of good instructors, the regiment was on the move again. By now we had learned the army's special language, for example: entrained/detrained, embarked/disembarked, emplaned/deplaned, marched in/marched out, and so on.

From our training camp we marched out to Amiriya, to more sand, dust and wind. We put fly nets over our heads while eating, which helped to deter some of the millions of flies, but there was nothing we could do about the wind.

The wind had a name, *Khamsin* in Arabic. It means fifty, because this hot southerly wind blows sporadically for around fifty days across North Africa and the Arabian Peninsula, usually during March and April. On bad days the dust reduced visibility to nil, and it was so strong that it sometimes blasted a vehicle's paintwork back to bare metal. The sand impregnated everything, and the only thing to do was to go to bed until it blew itself out. It got into our eyes, ears, hair, clothes, equipment and food, and there was always a massive clean-up afterwards. The dust storms in Saskatchewan, bad as they used to be, were just breezes in comparison. It was something everyone had to endure.

In April I was made a driver mechanic with the 68 Light Aid Detachment (LAD). Each LAD was an independent unit of one officer and twenty to thirty men, which could be assigned to provide repair and recovery support to any unit in the army. We were far from the fighting, and mainly did routine maintenance on trucks and other vehicles. The artillery did a lot of practice firing, which sometimes led to repairs on the guns. We wondered why we were there, and later found out that the regiment was supposed to support a British infantry brigade that had the job of defending Egypt against a threatened aerial invasion by Germany after the fall of Crete.

Fortunately, the German attack didn't eventuate, and in late June we began a long journey north to Syria by road. Over that week we travelled through places rich in history that I had read about and couldn't believe I was seeing for myself. Cairo was our first stop, and we camped under the pyramids of Mena, which they now call Giza. At night, most of us headed for Cairo's hotels and dance halls and spent a good while sampling what the Arabs had to offer. A demon drink called *Arak*, which tasted like aniseed and was supposed to be mixed with water, turning it a milky white colour, and then sipped. But it was cheap so most of us just upended the bottle for a swig and had sorry headaches from it.

We travelled onto Tahag, where we spent a day acquiring additional equipment. Then we travelled through Ismailia, across the Suez Canal and east across the Sinai Desert. Our ten-mile long mechanised column journeyed for two days to set up camp at Beit Lid. We had to stop regularly so that the leaders could walk away from their vehicles to take magnetic compass bearings. Despite everything looking the same, they kept us on the right track to Beit Lid where the LAD carried out a complete maintenance of the trucks and checked the stores before our next stop.

The column pushed north and halted at Matulla, on the Syrian border. We could hear allied and enemy guns in the distance. Our regiment was fighting the Vichy French who operated under the direction of Nazi Germany. For ten days we pounded the Vichy troops who lived up to their reputation as fighters. Fortunately our unit didn't suffer any casualties. There were plenty of near misses, though.

The LAD workshops were set up a few miles behind the fighting units under huge tarpaulins. Teams were sent forward daily on recovery tasks, or to return repaired equipment to a frontline unit. Sometimes we'd send a salvage team to find equipment that might be beyond economical repair and take parts off it to fix what we had in our workshops. Most LAD men were civilians with little military training, working on adapted civilian equipment. For example, we strengthened the chassis of our three-ton lorries and replaced their usual dual tyres with single large tyres.

We did have high morale and willingness to do our best, and our successes were due to working as a team. The LAD was self-contained. We carried our rations, cooking gear and arms. We lived on those trucks. Some trucks had lathes, drills, grinders, and welding gear. Also, part of the unit were the recovery wagons with powerful lifting and towing gear.

We also had to keep the roads clear for other vehicles. It was a bit like a military version of a roadside service callout. If anything took more than an hour to fix, the mechanics sent it back to a static workshop. Because of the lack of spare parts, we did a lot of improvisation. When we needed an electric drill, we cobbled one together out of a variety of truck and machine gun parts.

The Vichy French had an agreement with the Germans which gave them access to military facilities in Syria. They used Syrian railways and airfields to support their war and to attack the allies. The British forces conducted Operation Exporter, an invasion of Syria and Lebanon, in June and July. On 10 July, as the 21st Australian Brigade was on the verge of entering

Beirut, an armistice was signed with the Vichy French, and things quietened down for a little while.

We had a few days to rest up, then travelled to Aamiq to take part in the occupying force in Syria, to 'show the flag' and disarm and demobilise the Vichy troops. We travelled for sixteen hours over mountain ranges, along the edge of deep ravines, through Arab villages and around broken bridges, arriving at midnight. The regiment joined the British Borderers and Durham Light Infantry regiments. The LAD was busy keeping all vehicles roadworthy.

Dawn Patrol, Culver on right, 1942

Aamiq was built on a flood plain of the Litani River and was infested with malaria-carrying mosquitoes. Four-fifths of the unit became infected, including me. It didn't stop my friends and me from enjoying ourselves when we had precious days off. We'd take treks down the valley along beautiful mountain roads and through the villages. We'd trade bully beef with the local villagers for eggs and fruit to eke out the ration of biscuits, bully beef, margarine and marmalade.

On 6 August, we moved north to Baalbek with its ruined Roman temples and rich history. Everyone in the unit had permission to take an afternoon off and visit the ruins. From there we travelled for two days through an ancient land of mosques, ruined castles, aqueducts and large waterwheels to Aleppo, where we were stationed for the next six months. Aleppo is a twelfth-century city in north-western Syria about thirty miles from the Turkish border. Once one of the richest cities in the world, culturally, socially and economically, it is dominated by its Citadel, a medieval fortified palace.

As we passed through the city's edge, the local population lined the streets in silence. The regiment was the first AIF unit to visit the area since it had been occupied by the Vichy troops. We found out later that before our arrival, the locals had been told we were 'Menzies' Bushrangers' and we would cause trouble. The Vichy troops had bothered the locals, and so the locals were uneasy, as they didn't know what to expect from us. The women weren't taking any risks and kept well hidden in their homes. Once they realised we weren't going to be any trouble, they gradually returned to the streets.

In August 1941, I was promoted to Lance Corporal. This

meant I had a team of four to supervise as well as my usual work for the LAD. Besides keeping all vehicles roadworthy, we had to carry out guard and sentry duties in and around Aleppo. We took advantage of our leave time to explore the city. We visited the medieval Citadel in the old part of the city and the covered markets, or *souks*, which were full of colour and mystery. A popular venue was Madam Lola's with its belly dancing and exotic Arabic music, and some of the men spent a lot of time there.

Winter of 1941 was ushered in by torrential rain, driving sleet, snowstorms and intense cold. Solid gravel roads and vehicle and gun parks for the camp area became a priority before the temperatures dropped and the ground froze hard like concrete. Those who had removed the windscreens from their trucks at Beit Lid because of the heat, now deeply regretted it. As a measure against the cold, the Australians consumed large jugs of Jamaican rum, given out as part of our rations, and the hangovers were at a record. Even those who usually practised total abstinence glugged it down. It was so bitterly cold that we slept in all our available clothing just to keep warm each night.

Now I'll tell you how I received my one and only war wound. One night, some friends and I lit a fire in a 44-gallon drum, using sump oil as a starter due to the lack of available timber. We threw in what combustible rubbish we could find and sat close to keep warm. Some beer may have been drunk, just a little. As we were sitting on upturned kerosene tins around the smoking drum, some smart-aleck thought it a joke to throw a .303 bullet in. It exploded and I fell off my seat with a burning pain in my thigh. A nearby medic with a first aid kit was called for. The wound was fairly deep, but he removed the bullet with a pair of tweezers and applied a dressing. A court of enquiry was held, of course, but found it to be an accident. I still have an impressive scar on my leg.

At the beginning of 1942, the regiment and units heard the unsettling news of the growing threat in the Pacific. Thousands of Americans had 'invaded' Australia. The thought everyone had now was, *when are we going home?* On 7 February, after a rushed preparation, the regiment moved out on a long journey south, by road—destination unknown. On the first day, the long convoy passed through Hama, Homs and Tripoli. The next, along the coast of Lebanon, through Beirut and across the border of Palestine to Haifa. We arrived at Gazzah, south of Tel Aviv, to the news of the fall of Singapore to the Japanese.

The regiment spent the next three weeks refitting and preparing for a sea voyage. Though the destination was still unknown, rumours flew about and every place, except the South Pole, was mentioned. Before moving out, we had an opportunity to make final visits to Jerusalem and Tel Aviv. The new Jerusalem was just like any other modern city, but Old Jerusalem, built inside a wall, was an eye-opener. There were two highlights for me. The first was the Church of the Holy Sepulchre, where gold and silver lamps burned night and day, and we watched in contemplative silence, making our own private prayers. The second highlight was the place of the crucifixion, the actual site of the Cross marked out with a silver star, and a nearby statue of the Virgin Mary covered in jewels, watches and chains, which was worth millions of pounds, or so our guide claimed.

On the 6 March 1942, the regiment moved out in two groups to Suez. The LAD went with the vehicles and guns, the rest travelled by rail in cattle trucks. The main body of the regiment detrained at El Qassasin, in Egypt, and didn't meet up again with the LAD until April, in South Australia. The LAD boarded the *Glenpark* again at Tewfik, and we raised anchor, headed south and down the Red Sea, bound for Australia. The ship was travelling alone and unescorted, relying on speed, four 5-inch naval guns, and numerous ack ack guns for protection.

A field gun, 1942

Culver (second from right) with friends, 1942

Living conditions, 1942

Baalbek, Lebanon. Culver on right, 1942

War Years: Return to Australia and Papua New Guinea 1942

Culver on right, 1942

Once we were at sea, we found that the *Glenpark* had insufficient lifeboats and life rafts for the number of men on board, but fortunately it was an uneventful run, and the inadequacy was never tested. The journey was tedious, without the same anticipation we had felt heading into the Middle Eastern war, although we were all keen to see Australia again. The most boring job we had was lookout duty, but we were entertained by some of the infantry. They held competitions stripping their Bren guns, then reassembling them while blindfolded. The fastest one to do it won the cash bets that we laid.

Finally, twenty-seven days out from Tewfik, the Rottnest Island lighthouse came into view. Soon we heard the welcome sound of the port anchor rattling through the hawsepipe. Our captain ordered that only those who had enlisted in Western Australia would be granted shore leave but, to his surprise, it appeared everyone had done so, and as there wasn't any proof to the contrary, he couldn't stop the flood of returning soldiers pouring off the ship.

Our final destination was Port Adelaide, and when we docked, lumpers came on board to unload the trucks. Things were going well until they found out we had ammunition on board. At lunchtime, they walked off, demanding danger money to keep working. This was too much for some of our men, so they took over the winches and began the unloading themselves.

By that evening, shore leave had been granted, but no passes had arrived. A nearby pub beckoned. As usual, the standard form of exit, pass or no pass, was ignored and a large hole in the wire fence, close to the ship's gangway, suddenly appeared. The pub's beer ran out that evening due to the unexpected arrival of so many thirsty drinkers. No one wanted to leave, hoping more beer would miraculously appear, and when it didn't, tempers became frayed in the crowded bar and a near riot developed. Eventually, everyone came to their senses and, as discipline and common sense took over, everyone made a quick exit and stumbled back to the ship.

The next morning, the unit travelled by train to Angaston, in the Adelaide Hills, to wait for the arrival of further guns and equipment. I started to feel ill and quickly came down with a bad bout of the malaria I had first contracted in Syria. Soon I was back in Adelaide, in a military hospital, where I alternated between sweating and shivering and extreme thirst. Headaches and backaches added to my general malaise. It was something that sporadically appeared for the rest of my life.

The normal treatment would have been quinine but the world supply of it was largely under the control of the Netherlands which was occupied by the Nazis. The Dutch colony Java, the main source of quinine was occupied by the Japanese. I was treated with Atebrin instead, a powerful antimalarial drug, but it had some nasty side effects—mainly nausea, headaches, and diarrhoea. I missed the three weeks in Angaston which, from all reports, was remembered as one of the regiment's most pleasant periods. All were billeted in homes of the townspeople and nearby farmers, where all ranks were shown a generous hospitality.

In mid-June, the regiment packed up and moved by rail to the Stanley Ranges near Esk, in Queensland, for three months training. We in the LAD travelled by road with our trucks and mobile workshops, through the backwoods of Victoria and Central NSW, 'doing over' all the pubs and dances along the way.

The three months of jungle training was not too hard for the LAD, as our jobs were basically the same, and the weather was cool. After the training we were all sent for a two-month rest period on the coast at Maroochydore. That was a great time. We swam in the surf, ate all the tropical fruit we wanted and held night parties on the beach. These became wistful memories when we were sent to a camp near Caboolture for Christmas. It was in a low swampy area, and we endured heavy rain, mud, mildew, and mosquitoes. It was there that I received an order that would change my war, and my life, completely.

Culver on right, with LAD truck, 1942

Port Moresby
1943

Culver on left, hotel lunch, 1943

Rubber was considered vital to the success of the war effort, and with the retreat of the Japanese along the Kokoda Track, the government wanted the plantations back in production as soon as possible. Many former planters were being released from army service to make this happen. I got news of my posting at the end of 1942 and was sent on seventeen days leave.

Then, in early February 1943, I flew from Townsville to Port Moresby in a DC-3 that was being operated by the 21st Transport Squadron of the US Air Force. They certainly knew the route, as all they did was fly back and forth between Brisbane and New Guinea and points in between.

As I rode a Jeep in from the airfield, I could see the town had changed from the sleepy backwater I'd left two years earlier. There was continuous traffic of Jeeps, trucks, heavy lorries and motorcycles. The trucks belched clouds of exhaust smoke as they delivered their cargo to supply depots, ordnance stores and workshops strung along the muddy Sogeri Road. They came from the docks, where labour gangs were streaming up and down the gangplanks, their ramis tucked tightly into waists as they transported ammunition, tinned food, blankets, building timber, corrugated iron, spare parts, pipes, wire and machinery. Heavy trucks, loaded by crane, carried steel matting for airstrips and roads, large timbers for engineering works, aircraft parts and so on. Water and petrol tankers, road graders, ambulances, and tow trucks added to the general noise.

It was no coincidence that I was reporting to Mr Loudon, now a major with the Australian New Guinea Administrative Unit (ANGAU). His offices were bustling with uniforms and activity. He greeted me enthusiastically and quickly outlined the situation. Although the Japanese had been pushed back from the Kokoda Track, there was still fighting in the region. The activity at Port Moresby was to support the fighting around Lae and Wau and further along the northern coast of PNG. He said that there were still regular air raids, as the Japanese understood the logistical importance of Port Moresby. This was later made clear to me when they hit the town with at least a hundred planes in a raid in mid-April 1943, but by then I was back up at Sogeri.

Port Moresby had no white civilian population. All able-bodied, white male British subjects between the ages of eighteen and forty-five had been obliged to present themselves for military service. All other males, along with the women and children, had been evacuated. Then, after the town suffered its first air raid in February 1942, General Douglas MacArthur had placed all Australian and US Army, Air Force and Navy in the Port Moresby area under the New Guinea Force. Mr Loudon explained that the army had assigned a unit to help keep the plantations in order by clearing the fast-growing jungle and keeping the remaining Japanese out. Because labour was scarce, recruitment was one of my first jobs and ANGAU would help with that by hiring workers from the coastal communities and local villages.

As well as rubber production, my job included overseeing the growing, harvesting and delivery of whatever fruit and vegetables I could produce up on the plateau. Our most urgent customers were the hospitals, then the convalescent troops, and lastly, the casualty clearing station in Moresby.

The Australian Army had two big market garden schemes, covering one hundred acres on the banks of the Laloki River, twelve and fourteen miles north of Moresby. These produced Chinese cabbage, carrots, radishes, parsnips, tomatoes and snake beans. The Sogeri Plateau, about twenty-six miles from Moresby, would supply the fruit needed. Until these crops were available, everyone depended on vegetables shipped or flown from Brisbane.

A big change since I had left PNG was that the army had built a four-and-a-half-mile, fully-operational road up and over the Rouna pass to the top of the range and on to Sogeri, to support the Australians in their fighting along the Kokoda Track. This replaced the mule track we were so familiar with. Mr Loudon also filled me in with what his son, Ian, was doing with his Kittyhawks, which were ground-attack fighter aircraft.

Mr Loudon counted on Ian taking over the plantation business when he retired. Mr Loudon was one of the major planters in the district, and some people said that his initials, GA, stood for God Almighty. Ian was a friend, though seven years younger than me, and a real livewire. He was popular and capable at anything he set his mind to.

I knew Ian had followed his dream of flying by joining the Royal Australian Air Force (RAAF) in 1940, then volunteering to fly Spitfires with the British Pacific Fleet's Air Arm. In mid-1942, he transferred to 76 Squadron and served in PNG on Kittyhawks. Ian's squadron was commanded by Keith (Bluey) Truscott, who had also flown Spitfires in England. On one of his missions, Ian led a formation of Kittyhawks in an attack on Japanese planes sitting on the ground. Swooping in at low level, in multiple passes through intense anti-aircraft fire, they destroyed three Japanese aircraft. For this, Ian won the Distinguished Flying Cross. Mr Loudon was justifiably proud of his son.

In February 1943, just as Mr Loudon was telling me this story, the 76 Squadron was moved to a quieter posting in Western Australia where they maintained their training.

A short time later, Ian and Bluey made a mock attack on a low-flying Catalina. The sea was dead calm, perfect weather and unlimited visibility. The Catalina was slightly below them when Bluey started a shallow dive to intercept. Ian followed. Bluey was about fifty-five yards ahead of Ian, and the Catalina was about 765 yards ahead of Bluey. Ian noticed a fish jumping out of the water just in front of his aircraft. He suddenly realised that he was almost on the water.

He immediately pressed his transmitter button and called, 'Look out!' As he spoke, he pulled up steeply. At the same time, Bluey's aircraft hit the water at an almost flat angle. It bucked along the surface for about fifty-five yards, lifted out of the water and came up past Ian. It then stalled and dived almost vertically into the sea, narrowly missing Ian's aircraft as it fell. The plane sank immediately leaving a huge patch of flame on the water's surface. After Bluey's death, Ian became the youngest commanding officer of the 76 Squadron. Aged only twenty-three, he had progressed from pilot to squadron leader in just fifteen months. It was one of the fastest promotions on record in the RAAF. Of course, I only heard about this from Ian after the war.

At first light, the morning after I arrived in Port Moresby, I could hear the transport planes screaming like fighter aircraft as they took off from the nearby Kila Kila, Jackson and Wards airfields. Mr Loudon had warned me of the changes I would see. The military had confiscated all the houses. Koitaki, a plantation owned by Colin Sefton, had been requisitioned and turned into a military hospital. The Loudons' Eilogo homestead was now a convalescent hostel for wounded soldiers.

I took a tent and supplies and hitched a ride with an army truck travelling up to Sogeri. The Snake Road from Port Moresby to the Sogeri Plateau had become a lifeline for the Australian forces and the movement of military supplies. Dozens of Australian units (and some American units) camped along this road and its side tracks between 1942 and 1945. These units included engineering, ordnance, signals, survey, transport, medical and convalescent units, depots of ANGAU, and the Papuan Infantry Battalion.

I noticed the 7 Mile Drome (which later became Jackson Airport) had its existing airstrips lengthened and lined with steel matting—to stop the planes from slipping off the runways or sinking into the mud during the wet season, I supposed. There were also three new airfields, known as 12, 14 and 17 Mile, to intercept Japanese war planes heading for Moresby. These way-points were named as such because they were that distance from the capital. All the airfields had tents pitched half a mile from the runways. They were used for troop accommodation and were guarded by Australian soldiers.

The main road was heavy with traffic. Road graders, trucks, ambulances, Jeeps and motorcycles competed for road space. It could have been peak hour in Sydney, or holiday traffic returning from a long weekend, except for the vehicles' uniform drab green and khaki, and the deep-tanned drivers' outfits—khaki or jungle-green trousers and slouch hats.

At 14 Mile, I stopped off to inspect the market garden and citrus orchards the army had set up next to a hospital. The 160-acre garden on the banks of the Laloki River had its own irrigation system, and was maintained by local labour. The vegetables flourished in the tropical heat. There was a good range of produce, full of much-needed nutrition. These gardens provided between 10,000 and 15,000 daily rations for injured troops and others in Port Moresby. Nearby, at 11 Mile, was the Army Services Corps headquarters. That corps alone had several workshop platoons, eight transport platoons, two supply platoons and a relief driver platoon. They were responsible for maintaining all the vehicles and delivering food rations, oil and petrol to all units in the Port Moresby area.

With the gardens inspected, I hitched another ride and saw several gangs of soldiers, stripped to the waist in the energy-sapping heat, working on a bridge and causeways over a leech-infested swamp—an obvious mosquito breeding site. The once-green hillsides now showed massive red scars where bulldozers had cut out the earth to build the new roads. Further on, at 18 Mile, was the ANGAU Depot and the Native Labour Office. The office, which I would have a lot to do with, recruited local labour for the plantations and military units and liaised with the tribesmen who'd been recruited as guides and scouts.

Another mile on from there was a large camp of soldiers working for a Light Aid Detachment. The workshops were covered in camouflage netting. Their various jobs were ones I was very familiar with from my time in the Middle

East including vehicle maintenance, erecting buildings and collecting timber for structures. Some were assembling prefabricated metal buildings, while others went into the bush to cut timber for the engineering workshops. As we climbed the valley, the characteristic black volcanic boulders of the Sogeri district appeared, scattered across the slopes. We drove around the first S-bend, or Devil's Elbow, as some called it, then continued as the road twisted its way around the mountainside until it brought us to the top of Rouna Pass, and we caught a glimpse of the falls as we drove past and onto the Sogeri Plateau.

At Sogeri I said goodbye to the truck and collected the Jeep Mr Loudon had ordered for me. The area was full of Australian Army Service Corps personnel, whose job was to receive food from the Bulk Supply Depots and divide it into rations for units within the area. I took the road to the Mororo and Eilogo plantations. My heart rose to see the familiar forests of rubber and woodland. At various points I paused and took in the views of the towering Owen Stanley Ranges to the left, the Astrolabe Range to the right and, directly ahead, Mount Sogeri and Griffiths Sugarloaf.

The army had done an excellent job of maintaining both the Mororo and Eilogo properties. After arranging to have my tent set up at Mororo, I visited the factory to check the machinery. I could see it wouldn't take much to get it all going again. I radioed my labour requirements, and within days my workforce arrived. The collection and processing of rubber could begin.

Collecting the latex from the trees used a method called 'tapping'. It involved gently chiselling a V into the tree's bark. Milky fluid, latex, then oozed out and dripped into tin cups tied to the tree. When the cups were full, they were tipped into a small tanker towed by a Jeep and driven to the factory for processing. The latex was poured through a sieve into a large vat where clean water was added to break it up. Adding acetic acid coagulated the latex. This was left overnight in shallow dishes to form a thin sheet which was passed between two rollers and left to dry. Once the sheets were dry, they were carried to the smokehouse to hang for about ten days, then pressed together, weighed, packed in bales and sent down the track.

The whole process of latex production, including its tapping and collecting, proceeded with rostered teams around the clock. The collection of harvested food and its distribution also went into full swing. In some ways, little had changed since I'd left. The Japanese had come within eight miles of Eilogo, trying to push south to capture Port Moresby. Though the army people seemed confident the Japanese were gone, the occasional gunfire I heard in the distance had me praying they were right.

Tropical storms usually heralded the wet season and one night in October, the plateau experienced a beauty. The winds screamed through the trees, bending the tops with ferocity. Lightning cracked open the sky with the boom of thunder and on its heels came the rain. I heard a brief roar of engines and a loud crash through the storm's noise. With the help of some soldiers, my neighbour and I were on the scene as quickly as possible. We saw a swathe of treetops slashed and ripped by the Catalina flying boat that had crashed through them. It lay scattered over the ground, the right engine, oil, and fuel tanks all burnt out.

When rescue crews arrived the next day, we learned that it was a United States Navy Catalina returning from a mission over the Pacific Ocean. With zero visibility, they were flying on instruments only. Perhaps they were slowed by headwinds, and thought they were already beyond the plateau and descending to the Port Moresby seaplane base. The impact killed all six people on board. Their remains were recovered and buried. After the war, their remains were transported to Hawaii and mainland United States for permanent burial.

Soldiers scratched an inscription on the propeller, along with a message for the crew who'd lost their lives. The propeller was later removed and taken to the Port Moresby War Museum. The plane is gone now. Over the years it disappeared, bit by bit, either ransacked or pilfered by souvenir hunters or people just wanting building materials. We later ran cattle on a separate property which we named Catalina, in memory of that plane and its crew.

Cattle at Catalina

Port Moresby
1945

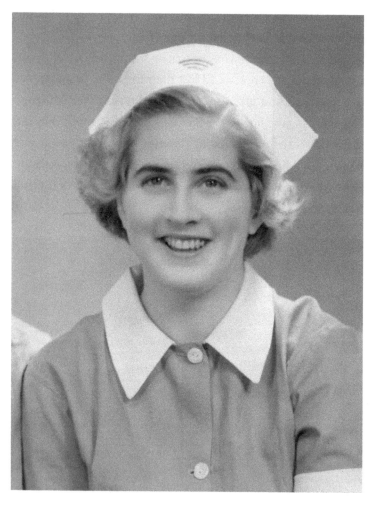

Margaret Anderson, Geelong Hospital, 1939

One day in July 1945, I parked a thirty hundredweight truck at one of the Port Moresby hospitals. It was loaded with crates of fresh pineapples, mangoes, starfruit and bananas that I had picked up from the army gardens beside the Laloki River. I loaded a trolley and trundled it across the dusty car park towards the hospital entrance. This was a voluntary task that I did regularly and enjoyed. It was lonely up in the mountains and the chance to chat with the medical staff was a welcome change.

Most other growers left the fruit with the matron, but I preferred to distribute it myself so I could talk to whomever I wanted. This particular morning, I was chatting with an orderly when one of the doctors called me over.

'Are you busy, Culver?'

'As always, but if you want to chat, I'm not that busy.'

'It's not me, but there is a patient of mine that I think you should meet. She is in the general ward with a broken leg. I think you two would get along.'

The doctor introduced Sister Margaret Florence Anderson to me. She was sitting with her left leg plastered to the thigh. A silvery band held back her soft waves of blond hair. I watched her smile, a deep dimple forming in her right cheek. She told me her broken leg had resulted from a Jeep rollover on the steep track up to Hombrom Bluff on a rare weekend off. Margaret and another nurse were taken on the trip by two army fellows. The driver was showing off and driving too fast for that road. I marvelled at her luck in avoiding a more severe injury or even death, as most of that track had a steep, rocky fall to the river below. She agreed, but also mentioned her regret at losing a treasured bracelet, a farewell present from her parents.

I promised to help find it for her when she had recovered. It gave me a reason to see her again.

I quickly learned Margaret was a skilled medical and surgical RAAF nurse—not the Medical Air Evacuation sort who flew in transport aircraft and carried pistols just in case they crashed in enemy territory.

Soon, instead of my weekly visits to Moresby, I was trying to find any excuse to visit Margaret as often as my busy job allowed. I plucked up the courage to ask her out to the pictures, and she agreed. We saw *Anchors Aweigh*, which was a lucky choice as she loved musicals. I'd been worrying needlessly.

One day, I suggested we picnic up on Hombrom Bluff and look for her bracelet afterwards. Hombrom Bluff is a rocky outcrop to the north of Port Moresby on the way to Sogeri. At an elevation of about 1,968 feet, it was (and still is) an extremely popular picnic spot with sweeping views of Moresby, the Laloki Valley and the coast. It was not too far from Moresby for a day excursion in the cool mountain air and got us away from the main Sogeri road.

After lunch I drove the Jeep part way back down the mountain and parked near the site of Margaret's accident. While she kept to the road's edge, I combed the rocks and gravel on the steep embankment. By good fortune, or divine intervention, I saw the sun reflecting off something. The silver bracelet was lying beside an ink-black rock. I called out to Margaret, holding it up in the sunlight. Both of us were astounded by the find. We had thought our chances were close to nil.

In August 1945 the Japanese officially and unconditionally surrendered to the Allies. Their navy had suffered four major defeats at the Coral Sea, Midway Island, the Solomon Islands in 1942 and the Battle of the Bismark Sea in 1943, which was the battle that broke the last major Japanese offensive towards Australia. The final blow for the Japanese came when America dropped an atomic bomb on Hiroshima on 6 August 1945 and another on Nagasaki three days later.

There was little to celebrate in Port Moresby. PNG had never received much consideration from the Australian Government, and this was still the case. Nothing close to normal could be achieved without available transport to return the civilian population home. There were also close to 150,000 Japanese in the islands who needed transportation back to Japan, and the same number of Australian soldiers to be brought back from Borneo, PNG, Bougainville and elsewhere. The appointment of a Civil Administrator didn't give us much early relief either. All planting, trading and transport activities were either carried out by the Production Control Board or those under their immediate control, and they were reluctant to relinquish control.

We were out one evening at the Officers' Club in town. Australian and American soldiers and nurses packed the joint. As a dance band played in the background, Margaret told me the RAAF had transferred her to the Heidelberg Hospital, an Australian Army Hospital in Melbourne. I was speechless. We had come to know each other very well over the preceding months and we were very close. I was hopeful for a positive answer to the marriage proposal I had planned. I sipped my beer, placed it on the table and held Margaret's hands in mine.

'Will you marry me, darling Margaret?'

It seemed like the silence stretched the minutes, as I waited for her reply.

New Beginnings
1946

Culver and Margaret Matley's wedding, Presbyterian
Church, Horsham, 1947

'You know I can't right now,' she told me.

She spoke so softly I thought I'd misheard. She shook her head, looked away and back at me. Well, that was a blow and not what I wanted or expected to hear. I leant back, pulled out a cigarette and lit it, inhaling slowly and deeply. I blew circles of smoke into the air. She continued.

'Our attraction is mutual, but the fact is, and you know it too, wartime romances tend not to last.'

I couldn't argue with that, but I said I wouldn't give up. We agreed to wait and continued to see each other until she flew out to Australia in November 1945.

After Margaret had left, my life got very busy because of political events over which I had no control. When ANGAU had taken over the administration and support of agriculture, the thousands of workers who had been indentured to the plantations were conscripted for army service or into crop production. Some villages lost ninety percent of their adult labour force, and their gardens had fallen into disrepair. This was alright while the workers were being paid £4 a year by the Federal Government, but soon after the war ended, it cancelled all their contracts. The result was near chaos as the workers all downed tools and went home. I didn't blame them.

The impact was as bad as that of the Japanese invasion. Almost overnight, production of copra and rubber dropped to near zero. Food shortages in the villages led to higher costs for plantations, which had to provide food to their workers at new, increased ration scales. While the workers ate well, the women and children in the villages were almost starved. Quite a few local businesses went broke. Everything imported came with a high duty that I don't believe was compensated by concessions on our personal income tax. Back in Australia, soap and margarine factories could not obtain copra and were shutting down.

I was demobbed in March 1946, which meant I continued doing much of what I had been doing, but now I was working and managing Mororo for Mr Loudon who had moved down to Sydney with his wife, Peg. His son Ian was back from the Air Force, where he had spent the previous year as chief flying instructor at a training school. Ian's time as squadron leader had given him a sense of authority and gravitas that was valuable in his role as manager at Eilogo. Together, Ian and I set about restoring the fortunes of the business. We were fortunate that we now had a good road from Sogeri to Port Moresby, and the villagers in our area had been familiar with our ways before the war. Further north, in the highlands, people had been dazzled by their first exposure to town life, cars, aeroplanes and American dollars. They were demanding a share of the perceived wealth and refusing to work under the old rules.

Australia had entered a trusteeship agreement under a United Nations charter, which committed to 'promote the political, economic, social and educational advancement' of the native population, and 'their progressive development towards self-government or independence'. We had to work out what the new rules meant and try to operate the plantation profitably. Apart from my work, I had continued my previous leisure activities—walking, listening to the wireless and weekend lunches and dinners with friends. I discovered reading! Well, of course I'd read before, but as I was on my own for much of the time, I became an avid reader and it helped fill the quiet hours. These things I now wanted to share with Margaret.

Margaret and I continued our courtship through weekly letters for a year until the anniversary of her leaving Papua New Guinea was coming up. I'd had enough. A year had passed, and she was still making excuses as to why she couldn't marry me. I sat down to write what I thought would be my last letter to her. I put my heart and soul into it, but I didn't beg. I sealed it with a soft kiss of hope and took it to the post office. Then a reply came …

> 5th November 1946
> My Dear Culver,
> Your last letter was a masterpiece, and it rocked me a bit. You know me too well and you have seen how I expected you to fit in with my little schemes. I thought I'd been so smart and evasive in my letters, but you've been a couple of jumps ahead of me all the time. You've written straight from the shoulder and have been completely honest as you always are. I see now how the land lies, and I love your pride. Anyone who can write a letter like that deserves only the best. You mentioned you hadn't much to offer me except adventure and I say I could be perfectly happy to join you up there, sharing the adventure together. The answer is yes.

Things moved quickly after that. I sent a telegram to my parents, with whom I'd been in regular contact through letters, with the good news, promising to give more details in a later letter. Margaret said she and her folks would organise the wedding. I just had to show up. We announced our engagement in late January 1947, and Margaret's friends threw a party for her in Horsham. I bought a gold Rolex watch from a jeweller in Port Moresby as a wedding present for Margaret.

It wasn't easy to get away. The rubber processing needed my close supervision. Though Ian Loudon was covering for me, I knew that the responsibility for Mororo's success lay with me alone. Dwindling copra supplies had been commandeered by the Government at £5 to £7 below world prices, and many plantations had been forced into bankruptcy. We were dependent on fresh food shipped in from Australia—any locally grown food was priced exorbitantly. Shanty towns had grown up around Port Moresby where villages had been destroyed during the war. Inland, the villagers said that they wanted to rebuild their villages before they would consider going back to work. The lack of coastal shipping made recruitment of labour almost impossible. I just had to put all of it out of my mind for a few weeks.

My flight to Melbourne took three days, with three Queensland stops before I arrived in Brisbane. I then took a direct flight to Sydney and another flight to Melbourne. I could have done it more quickly, but I wanted to catch up with the Loudons in Sydney. On arriving in Melbourne, I set out to buy a suit, as well as engagement and wedding rings. I knew exactly what I wanted and took my time to find the right ones. I walked up and down Collins Street, visiting every jewellery shop in the block, and then I walked into Drummonds Jewellers. On the counter, in a display case lit with bright lights, with a mirror amplifying the light, sat the ring I wanted. It was simple and elegant with a large diamond in the centre and a smaller one on each side, set in a silver band. There wasn't a price tag, nothing in there had one, so I had to ask. It was £135, a fortune, but I didn't care—I had money saved, and until now, there had been no need to spend it on anything substantial.

A tailor in the same block, Henry Bucks, had the suit and shoes I wanted, and all I needed now was a barber. I headed to the one next door, and he shaved my hair at the back and sides and slicked back the quiff with Brylcreem. I was ready.

The Overland train departed from Spencer Street and carried me to Horsham with my best man, my late Uncle Jim's son, Chris, who lived in Melbourne. Travelling through the vast empty Wimmera Plains, I was reminded of my hometown of Punnichy with its similar landscape. Margaret's brother Jack met us at the Horsham railway station and took us to a hotel. When I met Margaret's parents, I formally asked her father for her hand in marriage.

It was stinking hot that mid-February morning, not the best month to get married, but we had little choice, and Margaret knew I couldn't afford to be away for too long.

Someone placed a pink carnation on my lapel as I stood near the altar of the Presbyterian Church and wiped the sweat from my forehead. My throat felt dry, my collar tight. A beer would have settled my nerves, but my future in-laws were strict Presbyterians, and I knew the only choices would be soft drinks or tea. While I was standing at the altar, the organist quietly played Praise My Soul the King of Heaven. Suddenly, the Wedding March resounded through the church. The vaulted ceiling echoed the notes as the organist pounded the keys, and with each press of the pedal, the volume seemed to intensify. As the minister stepped forward, the music eased to a tolerable level.

I turned to see Margaret walking towards me, holding her father's arm with one hand and a bouquet of waterlilies in the other. A veil covered her face, held in place by a coronet of orange blossom. I could see her dimpled smile through the veil, and I was sure everyone could hear my heart pounding. Her mother's embroidered silk bridal gown fitted her slim figure perfectly. Following her were the bridesmaids, her sisters Mary and Jennie, wearing half-circles of matching flowers in their hair. I could see Margaret's influence in the flowers they carried— pink and blue hydrangeas, delphiniums and carnations—some of her favourites.

After listening carefully to the minister's words and repeating them, I placed the gold band on her left ring finger. With both hands shaking, I lifted the veil from my wife, Margaret Florence Matley.

Papua New Guinea: Mororo Plantation 1947

Margaret at Hombrom Bluff, PNG

We spent our first night as a married couple in the honeymoon suite at Craigs Royal Hotel in Ballarat. We had the Tower Room, and we climbed a short flight of stairs to drink champagne while we looked out over the lights of the city. After a long train journey and a week's honeymoon at Manly Beach in Sydney, we continued by plane to Port Moresby. I had promised Margaret an adventure, and so it proved to be.

Margaret was returning as a housewife, not a military nurse, and she said the drive to Mororo felt like a new experience for her. Despite the beauty of the mountains, she was still nervous when travelling on this road. There was a sheer drop to the river in places, and there were numerous rusting frames of military vehicles that had failed to take one of the turns. But when we passed the Rouna Falls, a sight you could never tire of, I knew we were nearly home.

As we approached Mororo, the rubber trees came into view; now tall enough that their canopies reached overhead across the road, the foliage so dense that the sun could scarcely penetrate. I had hired a cook, a gardener, and a cleaner and general help. Margaret was initially uncomfortable with this, and it took her some time to get used to having people in the house waiting on us. Hearing me talk to them in their own language was also strange as she didn't understand Motu. I assured her that I would help teach her the language. Having house staff to prepare our baths, take the covers off the beds and lower the mosquito nets were also new experiences. Margaret soon found that if she left any shoes or clothes lying around, one of the staff would whisk them away to be cleaned.

As everything was still in short supply because of the

troubled economy, much of our food came from tins. Fresh meat, especially, was hard to come by, but I shot the occasional pigeon or scrub turkey. There were plenty of wild pigs and cassowary in the plantations and jungle, and though they were considered delicacies to the locals, we didn't fancy them.

Margaret didn't want to sit around twiddling her thumbs, so she decided a vegetable garden would be her first project. She learned Motu too, enough to get by with the gardener and the house staff. When the housemaid became ill, Margaret found the right treatment in our medicine chest and put her right in a few days. Word spread quickly around the villages, through our house staff, that she had some medical knowledge, and soon village women began turning up almost daily with their infants and older children. Most cases were diet and hygiene problems, but there were also cases of malaria, dysentery, hookworm, leprosy and tuberculosis (TB), and Margaret enjoyed the work. The more serious cases went to Port Moresby for treatment. In return for her medical help, the mothers showed their appreciation with gifts of fruit and vegetables from their gardens.

The fresh food was invaluable. At this time, Port Moresby residents were living mainly on bully beef and sweet potatoes, plus whatever they could grow themselves, and we could get little from the stores. Butter was unobtainable, and sometimes there could be a month between boat arrivals from Australia. This made people angry, as the delays were caused by industrial disputes. This was having a serious impact on the rubber industry, and Lisle Johnston, manager of the Sogeri Plantation Company, remarked that we were better off during the war. Still, we made the best of our first Christmas together.

Mororo
1948

Matley home, Mororo

In 1948 we were still living in the thatched-roof and bamboo-walled house I had lived in since I arrived at the plantation in 1936. One morning, as I was helping a newly pregnant Margaret grasp some of the more complicated phrases of Motu, a foot-long centipede slithered down from the grass roof, followed by the unwelcome appearance of a giant green tree snake. Any remnant illusions of romance she might have had with that house were well and truly gone now. Uncharacteristically, she screamed and then let me have it.

'I want a new house,' she cried. 'One that doesn't harbour so much wildlife. I can put up with cockroaches, silverfish, ants and earwigs. I draw the line at repulsive giant centipedes and snakes.'

I couldn't argue with that. I would need plenty of timber, which I could obtain from the sawmill on the Eilogo property. I promised Margaret a roomy, timbered, iron-roofed house on our hill at Mororo overlooking the mountains.

Up until now I hadn't any serious labour problems to deal with until, one day at the sawmill, for some reason, things turned sour. I rarely had a problem with the local labourers, but when it did happen, it was an uncomfortable experience. On this particular day I was waiting by the Jeep for my team of four workers. Three tall, young, loose-limbed and cheerful lads climbed in, chattering and laughing and carrying their axes. Lagging behind was a fellow called Igua, who was frowning as usual. He was short, muscular, and darker than the others, both in colour and mood, and sat by himself. I knew that Igua was a sullen fellow and always too ready to pick a fight. Unfortunately, he had another year left on his contract, so I couldn't sack him without a just cause.

We drove about three miles to the Eilogo sawmill and pulled up by the sawpit. It was stinking hot, and my shirt was already dripping with sweat. It was only a two-person job, but I'd taken the extra two men to ease the workload because of the heat. The debarked timber had been positioned over the pit the day before, ready for cutting. While one of the lads took up his position on top of the log, the other jumped into the hole. Then they took the first cut with the long ribbon of notched steel. Igua dragged his feet after them.

Watching the men work the saw—moving up and down, up and down, bending their backs in unison—I noticed the set, sharpened and greased saw cut straight and true. It didn't run off the line, spoiling the timber. They were excellent craftsmen and careful workers. The top sawyer had to lift the saw at each stroke. It was hard work. The fellow below had it easier because the saw's weight aided the downstroke. But the pit job was the worse of the two jobs, because the pitman worked in a rain of sawdust which filled his ears and mouth. It would have been hard to breathe, so I wanted to ensure he wasn't in there too long. I directed Igua to stack the sawn planks while I checked on the next load of wood.

My absence was brief, but as I drove up, I noticed Igua sitting on his haunches, rolling a cigarette, the other men working flat out. I leapt out of the Jeep, reached Igua with a few quick strides, and curtly asked why he wasn't working. I admit I shouted and called him lazy, that I wasn't paying him to sit around, and ordered him to get back to work. Well, he jumped up, grabbed his axe and lunged at me. My army training was still fresh, and my reflexes were spot on. I grabbed his arm with one hand and twisted it until the axe dropped to the ground. I felt I was fighting for my life.

I picked up the axe, shook it at him and told him to return to work. The others watched the spectacle with amusement—it was a good excuse to stop work. As I turned to the other men to tell them the show was over and to get on with, it I sensed movement behind me. I spun back around to find Igua approaching with a plank of wood, ready to attack me again. Again, I knocked him to the ground. Both of us were now panting and dripping with sweat.

My heart was pounding, but I rough-handled him into the Jeep and called for the others to climb in, as they would be my witnesses. We drove for nearly an hour to the Sogeri Police Station, where I handed Igua over and made a formal complaint. When it later came to court at Rorona, he got two months in prison with hard labour.

Once I had all my timber, I could finally start on the house's framework, with the help of two local plantation carpenters. I had already surveyed and pegged out the corners and concreted in the foundation posts, selected for their termite resistance. Over a few weeks, working late into the night, we constructed crossbeams to create the framework. The kerosene lamps lured hundreds of moths and insects, and as they swarmed around the light, hungry frogs grabbed an easy meal. The various frog whistles, cackles, grunts and chimes almost drowned out the sound of the hammers.

Margaret was so keen to have a new garden she established one well before the house was finished. The house was built right on top of a hill so that from every window of the house there would be a fantastic view of the surrounding mountains.

I organised for all the trees a radius of about fifty yards to be cleared for her garden. She didn't waste any time and began planting bougainvillea, pale pink and blue jacarandas, yellow flame trees, various pines, palms, some tulip trees, almond nut trees, frangipani, poincianas, lemons and mandarin trees. At the edge of the garden, right around the foot of the hill, were the banana palms.

With the last of the roofing iron on, and with her garden already thriving, Margaret had about five months to go before our first baby was due. I assumed she'd go to Port Moresby to give birth, but she told me, no, she would have the baby in Horsham. Margaret wouldn't change her mind despite my arguments. She was adamant that the healthcare would be better in Australia. I countered that there were outstanding doctors in Moresby—Dr Stan Wigley, the TB specialist, for instance, whose wife Elaine would later be godmother to our youngest child. I also mentioned Dr John Gunther, commissioned as a flight lieutenant in the RAAF's Medical Branch, who became a tropical disease expert. He and his wife, Dot, were good friends of ours.

It was no use. I couldn't persuade Margaret. She would be with family, and I couldn't argue with that, so I booked her flight and Margaret flew south on her own for the birth. I couldn't afford the time off but knew she'd be alright with her family around.

The house was quiet without Margaret, and I tried to keep myself busy. If it wasn't plantation related, I worked on the house. I wanted it finished before my family returned. I missed her dreadfully. Margaret's weekly letters overflowed with news of family and Horsham. But as the weeks went by, and the Wimmera sun climbed higher, she started to mention how she missed the cool of the mountains and that she was experiencing some homesickness. Most of all, she missed me. I wrote of my longing for her, and the progress I was making with the new house so it would be ready for her return.

I continued with the house and put built-in cupboards in the kitchen, bathroom and bedrooms, and when the new stove went in, I had one last big job—to come up with a fully functioning bathroom—hot and cold water and the flush toilet I had promised Margaret. I decided on a donkey boiler I had seen on a ship years ago. Back then, the boiler system had powered the winches for loading cargo, but I realised I could use it to heat water, and it was simple to connect. The final touch was having the house staff polish the stained timber floors with coconut husks until they gleamed.

In those months, I was hardly aware, of the outside world. Australia was deciding whether Port Moresby should be the capital of PNG rather than Lae, Wau or Finschhafen. It seemed obvious to me that it would be Moresby, and so it proved to be. A radio telephone link had been established with Australia, so it might have been possible to book a call to Margaret from Port Moresby, but the cost was prohibitive, so we stuck with letter writing and telegrams. I finally received the telegram I was anxiously anticipating:

A girl, Mary Elizabeth 23rd February 1949, mother and baby both well.

I was very happy with the news, but what happened in Horsham and after the baby's birth is a story for your mother to tell.

Margaret's Story

Margaret Anderson

I was born in 1919, the fourth of eight children and grew up in Horsham, a farming town on the Wimmera plains of Victoria. Wheat fields stretched to the horizon, and in the Depression years the summers were scorching, with frequent dust storms funnelling through the streets on hot winds. I attended Morongo, a private girls school in Geelong, and on leaving in 1937 I began a nursing career at the Geelong and District (Kitchener Memorial) Hospital. After three years, I joined the theatre staff.

I enlisted with the RAAF Nursing Service in July 1942 and was posted to the No. 2 Hospital in Ascot Vale, ranked as Sister Group 2. I did further training at the RAAF Wing at Royal Adelaide Hospital. Then, as Sister Group 1, I had to complete a four-month course, including gas lectures, before being posted to the recruitment depot in Shepparton in January 1944. There I gave lectures on basic medical aid and the type of food to give injured or convalescing patients. Another duty was to provide all the necessary injections to the recruits. The depot needed a lot of straightening up, but I knew I would enjoy it, as I liked to work. When I arrived, the sick quarters were very dirty and the staff poorly trained, but it showed promise.

The first evening I was there the canteen fund held a dance. I went with another sister and eight officers. It got so hot towards the end that we went for a swim afterwards in the Goulburn River and stayed until about midnight. It was the best freshwater pool I've seen, situated right in the centre of town with a sandy billabong beach and floodlit. The food there was wonderful. The French chef in our mess made miracles from the army rations (and nothing else), and the RAAF had numerous fights to keep him there. The filet mignon with delicious vegetables was a poem. Breakfasts consisted of eggs, tomatoes and bacon, and every lunchtime we had iced coffee with a choice of mains accompanied by superb cold salads, all wonderfully cooked and attractively served. I spent eleven months there before the RAAF sent me to Laverton to prepare for my transfer to PNG.

When I first sailed into Moresby in early January 1945, I thought it looked much like the seaside town of Lorne in south-western Victoria. But Moresby was spread over a much wider area, and the coconut palms along the foreshore gave it a more tropical feel. The 21st Medical Clearing Station was formed in October 1943 and was responsible for evacuating patients from Port Moresby to the mainland, including civilians and Australian and American soldiers. I started work immediately.

Our CO was an ace surgeon, so surgery kept us busy as well as everything else. Most of my patients required frequent bedside nursing for scrub typhus. There was no known drug for its treatment. The symptoms were like malaria, with aches and pains, fever and chills and vomiting, and it was life threatening. Compared to the American nurses, we worked long hours. While they worked six hours a day, we worked eleven hours straight for two days a week and eight hours a day the rest of the time. We had fourteen days of night duty from nine at night to seven in the morning every six weeks, and only one day off.

Though we had little free time, we met all sorts of interesting people. These included the American Red Cross, flying nurses, missionaries, navy personnel and many others. Because there were so few females, we attracted a lot of male attention.

One memorable event was a dinner party on a naval ship. It was so rare and lavish, you'd have to have seen it to believe it. I dined at the captain's table with three other nurses, a colonel and his *aide-de-camp*, and the Air Force officer for the area.

On arrival the captain offered us Krug champagne, left over from his Singapore days. Damask linen clothed the tables which were decorated with silver cutlery and delicate crystal glasses. Ten Indian stewards attended the table of eight and the menu included, *soupe à l'oignon gratiné au gruyère, filet mignon* with assorted vegetables, peaches in chartreuse jelly, and fresh fruit. This marvellous evening ended with coffee, cigarettes and cigars. I'd never had such food, even in peacetime.

Of course, after my accident I became a hospital patient myself, and met Culver.

Horsham
1949

Soon after arriving in Horsham, I went to meet the doctor who was to attend the delivery of my first baby. My mother had made the appointment. When I entered the doctor's room, he stood to greet me and introduce himself. I saw how his dark eyebrows emphasised his amber-flecked green eyes and noted the smooth, unlined face. He looked like a young student, not a qualified doctor. When he kept flicking his head to get his too-long fringe off his face, my fingers itched to reach for the surgical scissors and snip it off.

He assured me he was well-qualified as a general practitioner. No, he didn't have obstetrics training, but he'd delivered plenty of babies, he said in reply to my questions. He admitted he'd only been in the role for a year but insisted I was in capable hands. His lack of experience concerned me. I had seen a lot of doctors, ranging from excellent to incompetent, and he would not be high on the competency list.

My labour dragged on for hours. The surges of contractions seemed never-ending. It was too late for the caesarean I knew I should have had. The doctor's mask was damp with sweat as he wrestled with the stuck infant. Crucial minutes ticked past.

Finally, I gave a desperate push and the doctor a final pull, then out slipped the baby girl, blue and still, with the umbilical cord wrapped tightly around her neck.

The doctor swore as he cut the cord, then used a syringe to gently suck the mucus from her mouth and nose. He grabbed a self-inflating bag as the nurse scooped my baby into a soft, warm towel. The doctor squeezed air into her little lungs watching her chest rise and fall. He pressed the bag until she dragged in a lungful of air, then another, and another. Slowly she turned a healthy pink colour. He gave her a gentle slap, and I couldn't help resenting it, though I knew he was just checking the Moro reflex and helping with the mucus. Her arms and legs shot out and she cried. I told myself that it would be alright.

We had agreed that if it was a girl she would be named Elizabeth, but from the start she was Beth. Beth couldn't feed properly and fussed with the nipple. Unable to latch on and suck, she whimpered continually. Finally, a nurse eased a bottle of Sunshine milk and water into her mouth. She enlarged the teat hole to let the milk flow more freely. Beth coughed and spluttered at first, but the milk went down easily.

After a few days, Beth's eyes started watering, and crusted mucus developed along her eyelashes. Tests confirmed what the staff suspected but didn't tell me until later—Beth had blocked tear ducts that would need surgery. My doctor came to tell me the bad news. He couldn't look me in the eye. Instead, he fiddled with a pen, cleaned his stethoscope, straightened his tie, then spoke with a rush. Beth was too newborn for the surgery now. It would have to be in six weeks, and the hospital would supervise the fasting period beforehand.

I was able to take her home to my parents' house, but six weeks later I was back at the hospital holding Beth against my shoulder. I paced the room, patting her back and whispering in her ear as I tried unsuccessfully to soothe the distressed, hungry baby. She had been fasting for twenty-four hours for the ten-minute procedure. Afterwards, as a starving, weakened Beth lay in the post-anaesthetic recovery room, she stopped breathing. The nurse responded immediately. Extra oxygen was blown into her mouth, along with gentle chest compressions, until she turned pink again.

By the time the doctor was satisfied to release us, I was so tired I barely had the strength to pick up the sleeping infant and carry her outside to my waiting parents. I did a fair bit of crying then, but Mother was a great comfort. The next day after lunch, Mother saw my exhaustion and insisted I have a nap, or at least a rest on a day bed out on the verandah, as the inside of the house was too hot and stuffy to be bearable. The day was still and silent, and birds were sitting in the shade with their beaks open. Mother told me what had happened while I was sleeping.

'I took the wee babe to the other side of the house, under the walnut tree, so we wouldn't disturb you. Beth was sleeping in her bassinet, and I was sitting next to her. With the midday heat, silence, and stillness of summer, I dozed off.

'The noisy exhaust of a passing car woke me. I checked on Beth and saw her lips had turned blue. I leapt from my chair, and blew gently into her mouth, again, and again, and again, until her little chest started to rise and fall.'

I never really knew the experience of being a happy new

mother. I was distraught, knowing that several bouts of oxygen deprivation could have a lasting impact. Highly anxious, I checked constantly on Beth. I felt guilty, knowing that she might have had a straightforward birth in the Port Moresby hospital if I had not insisted on travelling to Horsham. When I wrote to Culver I told him of the events but minimised my concerns about the baby. She seemed normal, and while she might need some specialist treatment, I had no real evidence that she had been harmed. Now I just wanted to go home to PNG with my baby and be with Culver.

Mororo
1949

Mororo, PNG

During my remaining time in Horsham I had a mothercraft nurse as well as my mother to help me with Beth's care, and I left with a renewed confidence in motherhood. My sister Mary agreed to travel home with me and stay for a holiday. We took a train to Melbourne and then on to Sydney, arriving on 1 June 1949. After some difficulties with our travel documents, we left three days later on the MV *Bulolo*, a passenger, cargo and mail boat which regularly sailed between Australia and Papua New Guinea. Mary would be the first family member to visit, and I was eager for the cruise to end. At three months of age, Beth was little trouble.

Culver drove to Moresby and stayed at a hotel the night before the ship was due to arrive and met us early the next morning. The Moresby wharf was the busiest it had been since the war. Lorries carrying six-foot logs from the Owen Stanley area jostled for position to be shipped south. Cranes and derricks of the eight-thousand-ton commercial ships nodded over the crowded wharf. Stores were piled on the jetty. Some were being loaded and others unloaded. Once we had cleared customs, everyone was keen to move away from the dirty, noisy and busy wharf. Culver drove us around the town pointing out the landmarks to Mary.

We showed Mary the barracks where I was stationed during the war, as well as Government House and the Papua Club. The latter was built on Ela Beach and later became the Public Library and RSL Headquarters. She loved what she saw of our little township. Everything looked glorious in the brilliant sunshine.

The shops weren't quite what she was used to back in

Australia. They didn't have display windows, and she said they looked like big sheds with large openings in front for ventilation. The Burns Philp store had another airing system consisting of six large, light-green canvas screens hung in parallel rows from the ceiling. The screens were connected by rods at the top and were weighted at the free end. The screens were powered by a small electric motor, and they rocked rhythmically back and forth in a slow, flapping motion. Everything it seemed, including the two theatres and hotels, was owned by Burns Philp.

Later that day we travelled on to Mororo. Mary had never been in a Jeep and her joy was evident. She wore a huge smile and her eyes shone as the wind blew her hair in different directions, and she could look straight up into the clear blue sky. We arrived at Mororo by nightfall, and I was thrilled by what Culver had done with our new home. He'd planted lawn around the house and with the tropical climate and rain, the lawn and the trees and the shrubs I'd planted months earlier were now flourishing.

Looking out the window on her first morning, Mary saw the hills around us were completely obscured by mist. The day gradually warmed up, and in the afternoon we had a soft rain shower. With the sunlight reflecting on a soft mist rising from the creek that flowed through Mororo, we could trace its course for miles.

The district was developing, too. A new school had opened in Sogeri. The buildings were an unlovely hodgepodge of thatch, cane, sisal paper and rusty reclaimed iron from army huts, but they were neat and clean. Even the Soviet and Ukrainian representatives on a United Nations visit had found little to criticise. Although I knew that just a few miles away the infant mortality rate was 40 times as high as the rate in Australia, I felt that Sogeri might be a good place to raise our family.

If I had been a new arrival, news of the conviction of two employees for the robbery and murder of Tom Bowes on his Laloki River property might have frightened me, but I knew this could happen anywhere in the world. There were much more dangerous places to live than the Sogeri Plateau. More worrying was a business crisis. Rubber was not selling because Australian manufacturers were refusing to pay Grade 1 prices for high quality rubber. The Planters' Association had advised members not to sell and as a result, stocks were building up in the warehouses. It was no exaggeration to say that the industry was facing disaster.

Within a couple of days after arriving at Mororo, Mary had her first encounter with the local wildlife. Dense undergrowth surrounded the house and harboured all sorts of creatures, and she saw a 17-foot black python come slithering out. She was in a state, crying and pointing until it disappeared into the undergrowth. Though the grass wasn't that high, Culver called in twenty tappers to cut all the grass around the house so as to steady everyone's nerves.

Mary and I quickly settled into a routine of days spent reading, sewing and taking walks through the plantation. Sometimes we chatted and gossiped about the family, and when Beth was awake we entertained her. On the weekends we had invitations to neighbours' houses for either lunch, morning or afternoon teas. We didn't need excuses to visit. One Sunday morning Culver had to return 'Bertha'—a three-ton truck—to Eilogo and collect some milk. We stopped and had morning tea in the trade store with Eileen Lukin and Margaret Loudon, Ian's wife. The tea-making facilities were in the office attached to the trade store, just a few yards from the main house. The stores sold a wide range of goods to both the plantation workers and to the villagers including rice, flour, sugar, tea, tinned fish, soap, clothing, blankets, kerosene lanterns, tobacco and matches. The prices charged were regularly monitored by both Native Affairs inspectors and the resident magistrate.

Our neighbours and good friends, the Johnstons, lived at Sogeri where Lisle managed the Sogeri Rubber Plantation, and his wife Eileen worked the trade store there. They became godparents to two of our children. Their home sat on a plateau, and in the early days, the Johnstons made their house available for the mobile clinics that visited to give whooping cough vaccinations.

A doctor named Joan Refshauge established the mobile clinics. Her husband had served in ANGAU during the war and had remained in Papua. Joan joined him in 1947, and the Department of Public Health asked her to establish an infant, child and maternal health service. She recruited staff, organised the training of indigenous nurses, and began school health services.

The mobile clinics she organised consisted of a doctor and trained sisters who visited the villages and settlements accessible by road. As well as regular health services, they provided powdered milk for village mothers who couldn't feed their own babies and tried to instruct them in the care and diet of young children.

Over the years, Joan established twenty-one central clinics, 528 village clinics and 541 centres visited by mobile patrols.

One Monday afternoon, Joan came up to Sogeri to give injections to the European children, but Culver had work commitments and couldn't drive us home. Eileen Lukin offered us a lift in her car. We climbed in with her two children and a local driver. I hated to be driven by anyone except Culver, but this fellow drove slowly and carefully all the way, and as we reached Mororo we all heaved a sigh of relief. It had been raining heavily for about an hour, and consequently, the road to the house was very slippery.

Because of the rain, the driver decided to bring us right to the back door, but unfortunately he didn't swing out far enough before driving up the embankment into the yard, resulting in the Jeep slowly turning right over on its side. We could see and feel it happening but couldn't do anything to stop it. Nobody was hurt. Mary was in the back nursing one of the Lukin children, and I was in the front, in the middle, nursing Beth who had been asleep until then.

Mary was wearing a yellow skirt and blouse she had made herself. She always had it dry-cleaned rather than risk washing, which might have ruined it. She'd been careful all the way home to avoid getting mud on it. By the time she scrambled out of the Jeep, slipping in all the surrounding mud, she was covered from top to toe. Six tappers had the car up on all fours within minutes, so Eileen and the children set off for home with an adventure to recount.

After the Jeep drama, Mary forgot to hang up her muddy clothes. On looking out her window the following day, she saw them hanging on the line. Rushing outside in a panic, she found neither her skirt or blouse had shrunk, nor had the colour run. She decided she would no longer need to have it dry-cleaned.

Mary had been with us for two weeks when Culver had to leave Mororo on a recruiting trip for new plantation labourers. Our labour force was employed on fixed-term contracts, so we regularly needed new workers. Culver would be travelling down to the Rigo district on the coast south-east of Moresby, and he'd be away for at least a couple of weeks. Since both baby and I had settled into a comfortable routine (Beth was feeding well on the bottle), Culver thought it was the right time to take the trip. He would not, however, leave two women alone at Mororo.

'John Lukin's brother, Langley, is visiting him from Sydney. I'll ask him if he is available and willing to stay here for a couple of weeks to keep you company,' Culver said to me.

John Lukin and his wife Eileen lived on Ninoa plantation, a few miles away. They were good neighbours and we had become firm friends. We'd met Langley at their place and found him delightful. Of course, I agreed.

The recruitment process involved Culver taking two men with him, one as an interpreter, and the other to carry. A carrier carried food, tobacco, newspaper and other things that might entice someone to sign up for work. It was more for goodwill than anything else. Plantation managers had widely established reputations among the villages and towns as to whether they were acceptable to work for, and Mororo already had a good reputation.

Culver and his assistants started their day at 7:00 am and

finished at 4:00 pm, stopping for a midday meal. They trekked many miles over rough terrain to the various villages. They spent their nights in rest houses built by the local villagers. These were simple shelters of bamboo walls, thatched roofs and dirt floors, erected to accommodate travellers and were built at intervals of about five miles along the tracks and roads.

Soon after Culver left, Langley Lukin arrived with his Jeep packed for a civilised sojourn with literally everything but the kitchen sink. For the expected two-week stay, he'd brought his dog, his cat, a Persian carpet (as he didn't like the feel of timber boards under his feet) his favourite books, a wireless, and quite a nice collection of records which Mary and I made good use of. He also brought his cooking gear, as he loved to cook, which raised eyebrows in more than one quarter of the household. He even brought his own pictures to hang on the walls.

A few days later, Langley drove us to Eilogo to collect some beef. The Seftons at Koitaki plantation had killed an ox the previous week, and we'd been offered about thirty pounds of meat from it. We enjoyed delicious grills and roasts, all cooked by Langley, which irritated our house cook Garse immensely. He viewed the invasion of his kitchen domain with suspicion and growing ill grace.

Though Langley was fun to have around the house, one night sitting down to the dinner that he had made, he went into great detail about how he prepared and cooked the sweet potatoes, the beef olives and grilled the steaks. Garse was already in a bad mood from having Langley take over the kitchen, and this was the last straw. The next day he voted with his feet and downed tools and apron. He stormed out, declaring that he wouldn't be back until Langley was gone. Bora, our young laundry man, taking stock of the situation, left in sympathetic support.

We had a young married couple turn up who looked like being the replacements we wanted, but they left too. The young man's father died, and they had to return to the village for the burial feast. They said they would come back, and in the meantime, we were reduced to two very helpful staff. Langley seemed more than happy to appropriate the role of cook. While Mary and I knitted in the evenings, we listened to him read chapters from *All that Swagger*. He had a beautiful voice that sounded like it was made for radio.

It was unfortunate that a serious incident took place in the time that Culver was away. Two Rigo tribesmen, on leave from Eilogo, attacked a Tufi near Moresby over a game of cards. The Tufis declared war, stamped their feet, sang war songs and beat their drums all night. The following day, two hundred men carrying spears and axes set off for Eilogo, passing along the road in front of Mororo. We didn't know what it was about and did not go outside to ask.

The Rigo tribesmen on the plantation warned Ian about what was to happen. They told him that the Tufi were well-armed with spears, so he phoned the Sogeri police who sent out five unarmed men to help him. Ian took his shotgun and the six of them surprised the war party on the road.

Twenty Tufi leaders came forward and thrust their spears back and forth at Ian and the police officers. The rest of the two hundred-strong war party stayed well back, waiting to see how it would play out. The perspiration ran down Ian's face, but outwardly he was calm. He pointed his shotgun at the group, calling them to drop their spears, but they kept moving forward, shouting and threatening. Ian called their bluff by raising his shotgun and firing into the air. The men immediately dropped their spears in fright, and the war party bolted. The police later arrested the ringleaders.

As you might imagine, we became anxious for Culver's return. After he had been gone two weeks, we received a radio message that Culver would arrive home the next day on the *Managoora*. When I heard the news, I had the staff flying in all directions cleaning windows, polishing floors and changing linen. John Lukin went down early that morning to meet the boat and waited all day until 6:00 pm. He telephoned to say that there was no sign of the boat—that someone at Burns Philp told him it had left Rigo, and that the boat's wireless had failed somewhere between Rigo and Moresby. John said he'd watched out the night until 10:00 pm, and then he'd gone to bed.

The next morning, there was still no word from Culver or any news of the *Managoora*. I was a nervous wreck imagining all sorts of things which may have happened to the ship. Silly Langley wasn't any help, saying the south-east season always brought high seas, and he pitied anyone caught out in such weather. Overcome, I held up a hand and then walked out of the room.

I rang the Burns Philp office twice that day. On my second call I was told they had received another radio message from Culver telling them he was arriving at 2:00 pm that afternoon. The *Managoora* had not left Rigo on the day it was supposed to, and Culver sailed in perfect weather enjoying a good trip. It was just awful while he was away, with no letters or communication. It made me appreciate him all the more, the way he looked after and spoiled us all.

When Culver walked in I couldn't believe his transformation. He looked so well—lean, very brown and rugged.

'Well look at you,' I said, hugging him and feeling his bones. 'What happened to that extra weight you were carrying?'

'Well,' he replied in that lovely Canadian drawl I'd missed so much, 'days of footslogging to remote villages on two meals a day might have something to do with it.'

'Did you get the men you wanted? You're back a little early. Not that I'm complaining,' I added as I hugged him again.

'Yes, I managed to hire twenty-five men, the most yet, but I ran out of rations for the carriers, so I had to cut the trip short. But I won't need to go again for some time.'

With Culver back home there was no further need for Langley to stay. He repacked his Jeep with all he'd brought and returned to the Lukins. As soon as he left, Garse and Bora reappeared, much to everyone's relief.

Mary's visit had filled me with joy, and I dreaded the day when she would have to return to Australia, but of course it arrived all too quickly. We drove Mary down to Moresby and the docks to meet the MV *Bulolo* for its journey south. I spent weeks afterwards missing her cheerful company and ready laughter. And for a while the house seemed sad as well, as if it too felt her absence.

Social Life
1950s

The new decade brought a sense of renewal to PNG. A tourist hotel was being built on the Kokoda Track, there was regular news about oil and gold exploration, and the rubber dispute, while not resolved, showed hopes of improvement. However, Japanese soldiers were still being found living with highland villagers, and the Port Moresby housing and wharf areas still needed a lot of work.

In 1951, like all the women in the district, I received a note from Mrs Unwin, the wife of the headmaster at the Sogeri Education Centre. The message read in part that local women could be assisted by a local Country Women's Association (CWA) because of the problems with distance and transport. As planters' wives, and wives of teachers and other expatriates, we all thought it a great idea and became enthusiastic members. It was a terrific way to socialise with people. I was nominated as the first secretary but declined after thinking it over. When I considered the work involved and my existing commitments at Mororo I decided it was too much.

Most of our socialising centred around the CWA and its fundraising efforts. We held our early meetings wherever we could find a place to meet. Sometimes we took turns hosting the meetings in our own homes, or in the downstairs room of the primary school or at the Education Centre. It soon became apparent this wasn't a satisfactory arrangement for either of the schools, or us. It was a topic we discussed at several of our meetings, and the solutions offered were never ideal. We decided that we needed our own dedicated meeting place. It took a lot of events to fundraise the money.

Eileen and Lisle Johnston generously donated a suitable block on their land at Sogeri plantation. Our husbands organised the building using local labour and several working bees, and we soon had a smart wooden building. It was terrific for our local meetings, but the Rouna Hotel was better for any larger social gatherings the CWA sponsored. It had the space and location, and when the CWA organised Melbourne Cup race days, the Moresbyites would drive up to the hotel in droves. It was a top-rated event.

My own involvement in the CWA was interrupted by the birth of our second child, Christina, in April 1952. Culver and I weren't taking any chances and he took me into Moresby, before my due date, to wait with friends. I had intended to have Beth with me, but they only had a single room with a single bed. It was just as well, I suppose, as the room was upstairs with lots of nick-nacks which would have been a temptation for a young child. She would have been bored in no time, and the heat was stifling. I couldn't sleep for the first few nights, but I got used to it.

The waiting was almost unbearable, and I was so sorry to see Culver and Beth go after their visits. I just wanted to be home with my family. Beth would be teary and tell me she didn't like the baby in my tummy. Culver said she was little trouble, and he was managing well with good help from a 'nurse girl' as we called her. However, he was taking Beth on his latex runs in the afternoon, so she wasn't getting her afternoon naps, and they both looked tired. Those eleven days seemed like forever, but Christina arrived on schedule and without complications.

The most significant fundraising opportunity for the CWA, apart from the movie nights, was the Sogeri Gymkhana held in conjunction with the Sogeri Agricultural Show. All the CWA members baked up a storm of scones, cakes, pikelets, biscuits and anything else we could think of for our stalls.

I was back into full involvement with the CWA when the first Sogeri Agricultural Show was held in August 1953 on the Sports Oval at Sogeri High School. It was so successful that the show quickly outgrew its space. Later, in 1957, Mr Sefton, the show president, donated thirty acres of Koitaki plantation land where they continued holding the show until 1963. My memories of the Sogeri Show from those years are all mingled now. I recall clouds of dust rising from the hundreds of cars taking people to the showgrounds. The line resembled an army convoy. Extra police from Port Moresby controlled the traffic flow at different points along the road, particularly up the winding Snake Road. More police at the showgrounds directed cars to designated parking areas.

The grand parade included horses, cattle and dogs. Thousands of people from the many tribes in the district mingled with about a thousand expatriates. Everyone dressed for the occasion. Europeans wore shorts or long trousers, dresses and hats, while tribal members, with their intricate facial and body tattoos, wore decorations according to their particular clan. For example, the Huli clan or Wig Men from the Southern Highlands decorated themselves with elaborate wigs made from hair to which they added birds of paradise and parrot feathers and splashes of red ochre. They painted their faces yellow, red and white. The Goilalas from Central Province added to the colour and excitement by wearing elaborate headwear decorated with birds of paradise feathers. The Asaro or Mud Men from the Eastern Highlands covered their skin in a grey and white clay, making them appear ghostlike. They wore oversized mud masks designed to shock and intimidate. They differed from the other tribes by being the least adorned and moved in slow, graceful steps, some carried spears, some bows and arrows, while others carried clubs.

Different tribes set up stalls throughout the showground area, selling the food they grew in their gardens and artefacts they had made. Banana leaves served as makeshift plates for the women who sold sugar cane, fruits and whatever else they grew. Others sold a wide range of wood carvings, from boats to masks, hand-woven baskets and traditional string bags.

Local groups would periodically take over the arena and hold a dance or 'sing-sing', as it was locally known, giving them a chance to show off their distinctive cultures through dance, music and costume. It was a huge drawcard, and the crowds jostled for prime viewing positions.

During the dances, women in grass and bead skirts, and men in tapa cloths carrying traditional weapons danced to the rhythmic beat of the drums. With the occasional war cry, the cheering and clapping audience drowned out the sound of bellowing cattle, neighing horses and barking dogs. The dancers were all reluctant to leave the central arena to make way for the polocrosse events, and when they finally did move out, most of the audience did too.

The CWA provided scones, small and large cakes, bread rolls and sausage rolls. The men manned the drinks, barbeque, and hot dog stalls and also ran the various livestock judging and the gymkhana horse events. Culver's job was to showcase everything produced in the territory, which involved quite a bit of his time. He'd set it all out on trestle tables: papaws, bananas, sugarcane, pineapples, mangoes and starfruit. On the ground were brown hessian bags full of bundles of tobacco leaf neatly tied together, plus smoked and baled rubber, coconuts and copra.

The Royal Papuan Police Band proved to be another drawcard in the central arena. Dressed in black *sulus* (a type of sarong worn from the waist down) and jackets with red piping, red cummerbunds and black berets, they were an impressive sight and played their tubas and trombones for the enthusiastic onlookers. The Police Force Training Depot at Sogeri attracted hundreds of recruits from all over PNG and the surrounding islands. They underwent intensive training to equip them for police service in any part of the Territory and their band was first-rate.

An Australian named David Crawley was the driving force behind the band. He had joined the PNG Police Force at Rabaul 1935. The band's first public appearance in Rabaul impressed the administrator so much that he released David from police duties to manage a police band. In 1942 he joined ANGAU, was transferred to the Police Force Training Depot at Sogeri and was requested to form a police band there. The band became very successful and later travelled to Australia. Their first tour was to raise funds for the Third Victory War Loan and this was very successful. They also played at the Sydney Anzac Day March in 1950, Queen Elizabeth's visits in 1954 and 1963, and the Melbourne Olympic Games in 1956.

As the show attracted most of Moresby's population, and the attendance numbers increased yearly, the management committee decided to move the show to Moresby in 1962. The Koitaki Club was at the end of a twenty-five-mile, single-lane, unsealed road, and with the extra show traffic on the road, it had become a traffic control nightmare, especially if the weather was bad.

On weekends, most plantations showed movies hired from the Moresby library, to entertain themselves and their employees. They were usually spaghetti westerns and Jungle Jim movies and were immensely popular. Sometimes, if money needed to be raised for a particular cause, something better was hired to justify the entrance fee. On one occasion the distributors donated the movie *The Cruel Sea*, a British war film starring the famous Jack Hawkins. We were raising money for the Hungarian Relief Fund. Nearly everyone from the district, as well as people from Moresby, turned up. Culver manned the door and collected the admission fees, which were five shillings for Europeans and one shilling for the local indigenous population. To accommodate a couple of deaf patrons, the fellow operating the projector turned the volume to the maximum. As depth charges sent vast water columns into the air, Jack Hawkins shouted out orders, while torrential rain on the tin roof drowned the sound. My ears were ringing as the final credits rolled.

In the early days, dinners and lunches had been held at various family homes, but the community wanted a central meeting place, somewhere to hold formal and informal functions. Plantation manager, Tom Sefton, offered part of his Koitaki plantation land to build a clubhouse, later called the Koitaki Club.

We held meetings to decide what we wanted, drew up the plans and then launched into action. The plantations provided labour and materials, and the plantation managers supervised and assisted in the working bees. Everyone worked together to get it built. On completion, we successfully applied for a Club License. The work didn't stop there. The committee also managed to install two concrete swimming pools; a large one for the adults, and a smaller one for the children. They also put in a cricket pitch and tennis courts.

Empire Day was a big occasion and a chance to dress up to the nines—the men in dark or white suits and the women in long dresses. It was a celebration of the British Empire and was held on 25 May, Queen Victoria's birthday.

The one we held in 1954 was on a warm, humid evening, and although we dressed formally, we had to be comfortable as well. Culver wore a grey linen suit, and I wore a blue organza strapless dress with a matching bolero jacket. The room was a sea of suits and dresses of silk, velvet and taffeta. Silver and gold jewellery sparkled in the candlelight, and everyone was holding either champagne flutes or pewter mugs of beer. A rami-clad waiter approached us with a tray of drinks—the choices were whisky, champagne or beer. A large photograph of the Queen dominated the scene and added a patriotic atmosphere. Everything displayed the British colours of red, white and blue; from the drapes to the flowers, all reflected and intensified by the large wall mirrors.

A waiter rang a loud bell to penetrate the rising noise level and announced the start of formalities. The master of ceremonies, Ian Loudon, rose to his feet and welcomed everyone. We paused for two minutes of silence in honour of fallen soldiers in both wars, particularly those who died on the Kokoda Track.

The sombre silence was broken by the voice of a kitchenhand, who everyone heard calling out to the chef. A head shake and a hiss from a waiter soon silenced him. At the end of the two minutes, the emcee led the singing of *God Save the Queen*, followed by *Land of Hope and Glory*. We then raised glasses to toast the Empire.

The emcee rang the bell again. 'I will say grace, and then dinner will be served,' he said, to the general relief of the guests who thought the formal proceedings were going on for far too long. The dinner reflected patriotic choices for Empire Day: Scotch broth, English roast beef, Yorkshire pudding, Irish potatoes and plum pudding, all cooked to perfection. Waiters served Australian wines, Scotch whisky and Queensland lager. Culver later said he would have liked maple syrup slipped in somewhere on the menu, but he'd kept the thought to himself.

The drinks came around regularly. After dinner, the crowd

moved out onto the verandah by the pool to watch the fireworks. Roman candles and Mount Vesuvius cones flared on the lawn. Jumping jacks bounced randomly, exploding at each jump. Catherine wheels of all different sizes spun on posts, throwing out showers of colourful sparks as rockets arched into the sky, bursting into colourful comets.

The Sogeri Plateau offered a cool escape from the hot climate of Port Moresby. Many celebrities and government officials of the day found an excuse to come up to Sogeri. Sometimes we would just bump into them in Port Moresby. Pauline Floyd was the wife of the engineer in charge of the new hydro-electric project at Rouna. Culver and I had met her when she was a singer with the Dick Bentley Show, entertaining troops during the war. She was a lovely, fun, natural person, and a good friend of mine for the time she remained in the district.

One day she came along with us when we travelled into town for supplies. When the time came to collect her, she was outside the hair salon with Chips Rafferty. At the time, Chips was a well-known and very popular Australian actor. Pauline introduced us to him and some of the film crew accompanying him, and he explained he was in the middle of making a film in PNG.

Tom Cole, a famous crocodile hunter, was an occasional visitor at the Koitaki Club, which was where we met him. He had been a successful horse breaker and buffalo hunter in the Australian Northern Territory, and had gone on to pioneer the crocodile-hunting business with a mate, Jack Gaden. They shot the crocs from a boat at night using .303 service rifles. They tanned the skins which were used for fine leather goods.

Although born and raised in Sussex, England, Tom was a very rough and ready character and hardly acceptable in polite society. He later wrote popular books about his life experiences.

Schooling was problematic in the early years after the war. The first classes for European students were held in the Church of England chapel of the Eworogo Convalescent Depot, which later became the Sogeri National High School. Many moves occurred before a permanent school was built in the early 1950s.

At Sogeri we had two primary schools, officially known as Primary A and Primary T. Plantation owners and managers built the Primary A school, with the community's involvement. It was a one-room, one-teacher school, built on stilts, with woven bamboo walls and an iron roof. The tall ceiling and the large windows helped keep the room cool. The administration provided a teacher for each school. Until a dedicated house was built for them, the teachers billeted with different local families, usually for a couple of months at a time.

Normally, the administration provided schools for children regardless of race. In general, Primary A schools enrolled European, Asian and mixed-race pupils while the Primary T schools enrolled indigenous pupils. If the indigenous pupils spoke English fluently, they could attend Primary A. The A school taught the Australian State Department of Education curriculum. The T school followed a curriculum for native schools in the Territory.

Until 1960, formal education for white children ended at the sixth grade. After this the children did their lessons by correspondence or, as the majority did, went to boarding school in Australia. The government provided a return airfare and subsidised attendance at an Australian school each year. There was an exam at the end of sixth grade that students needed to pass to be eligible for the subsidy.

Culver had an assistant named Graham Buckley. He and I took it in turns to transport our children to and from school. It was always more fun with Graham, the children told us much later. I was a nervous driver and always drove slowly. Graham was the opposite. He'd collect the children in his Land Rover from the top of our drive. They usually shared the ride with tappers who were being driven to different parts of the plantation. Once the vehicle hit the gravel of the school road, the children used to climb out the back and scoot their feet along the ground. They kept out of Graham's line of sight though.

At the school the children had grass to play on and were allowed to play in bare feet if they wanted to. They had bush to explore, and a shallow creek behind the school building in which they could paddle. The grounds also provided a habitat for pythons and other snakes, monitor lizards, insects; alternately fascinating and terrifying the children.

Most of the children's parents worked on the nearby plantations while the others came from the nearby Rubber Research Station and local cattle stations. We had a wide range of nationalities: Dutch, New Zealanders, Scots and Indonesians.

There was the occasional drama, and one such occasion occurred in 1965. As told to me by one of our children, Mrs Armstrong, the teacher's wife, appeared at the school door one day. This was unusual, and when she beckoned the entire class to follow her, the children were intrigued. She whispered that they were going 'on an excursion' and held her finger to her lips to signify they had to be quiet. They filed out of the room quietly, and excitedly. My daughter wondered, as did the other children, what was going on. They followed Mrs Armstrong back to her house, just across the road from the school. Even more alarming, Mr Armstrong stayed behind, just nodding to her as she led the pupils out.

Once they were safely inside the house, Mrs Armstrong played *The Sound of Music* on her record player to distract the children. She alternated between getting them to sing along and taking anxious looks out the window.

They didn't quite get to the end of the soundtrack before Mr Armstrong appeared and gave the 'all clear' to return to school, where they learned what happened. The Armstrong's cook had gone out in a rage to look for his wife. He had taken a long knife and was seen heading for the school. Mr Armstrong confronted the cook and talked him out of his rage. When he was calm enough, the man reconciled with his wife, and they both returned to work.

Tribal Matters

Worker tapping rubber

Tribal customs didn't change much during the time we lived in PNG, and the law still allowed a man to have more than one wife. The high price for brides usually discouraged the practice, however. It was also a form of insurance money for the bride's parents in their old age and encouraged the survival of female babies.

One day Culver was working down by the river when Garse, our cook, approached him. Culver had just finished clamping an irrigation pipe to the pump to carry water from the river to the house, as I wanted to expand the garden with another terrace and put in a proper fernery. We were experiencing a drought at the time, and I was going to need more water for a larger garden. Garse was dressed in his best white *rami,* with beads around his neck and frangipanis in his hair. It was apparent he had something important to tell Culver.

As it turned out, he was planning on taking a second wife. Garse was planning a big party in a month's time for his tribe, the Koiaris, and he wanted to invite Culver and me to impress his guests at the ceremony.

He told Culver he had only invited the boss boys and their families from the other plantations. The tribal custom regarding brides was that a bride price had to be paid to her parents. It sometimes amounted to hundreds of Australian pounds in cash, as well as articles of value such as shells used for body ornaments, and large quantities of food, depending on the social status of the bride and groom.

On the night of the party, which was to continue well into the next day, Culver and I lay awake most of the night listening to at least fifty drums thumping out their different rhythms.

We decided to spend the next day at the beach to escape from it, as we knew the festivities and the drums would go on all day. We had promised to visit and told Garse we would do so on the second day.

The party was still in full swing when we arrived after breakfast. Men dressed in their best outfits stamped their feet and sang to the beat of the Kundu drums. Voices rose and fell to the rhythm of the drums, grass skirts swayed in time to the beat. As most of the singers had been to the mission schools, the songs sounded like the black spiritual songs of the southern states of America; beautiful and mesmerising. Some of the partygoers had their thick frizzy hair combed and teased until it stood out about four or five inches, into which a variety of colourful bird feathers and flowers were placed. These included bright red hibiscus and the feathers of cockatoos and birds of paradise.

Everyone wore their best jewellery. Carved bone and shark-tooth necklaces hung from necks, while wood and tortoiseshell bracelets circled wrists and ankles. White bone was worn in pierced noses and earlobes. Intricately tattooed faces and painted bodies added to the party atmosphere.

Garse had arranged to slaughter one of his prize pigs for the occasion. It lay roasting in the earth oven while fish simmered in lime-coconut sauces on nearby fires.

As Culver presented Garse with a case of tinned fish, our contribution towards the festivities, Garse told Culver that his guests were already saying it was the best party they'd been to, and Mororo was the number one place to work. He led us across to two trees which had been cut down from the forest. Pound notes that the guests had given as wedding presents covered one of the trees. There was at least £50 pinned there, a good amount, and Garse couldn't keep the smile off his face. Draped over the other tree were wedding gifts of the best potatoes, yams, pineapples, mangoes, pawpaw, bananas and coconuts, all harvested from guests' gardens and the surrounding bushland.

One of the more stringent tribal rules was the tradition of payback—a blow for a blow, and a life for a life—and plantation brawls were frequent. They were partly caused by traditional tribal enmities, and by the fact that many men lived together on plantations away from their families and the usual customs and restraints of village life. Arguments often developed from trivial causes and were often disputes over the ownership of a piece of food, a cigarette, or over card games. The village men were hardcore gamblers. Quite often there'd be disputes between tribes, and Culver quickly learned to use tact and diplomacy so as not to let these incidents escalate. Usually, he had some warning before a fight or old pay-back was going to occur.

I have mentioned the incident involving Ian Loudon when Culver was away. On a separate occasion, two tribes rioted on the plantation, resulting in two men sustaining severe injuries. One ended up with a spear in his thigh, the other badly beaten up. Culver had to get them into the back of the utility and drive them to the hospital where they were successfully treated.

The next morning Culver and I were sitting down to breakfast when forty men marched past the house armed with axes and spears, to pay back the culprits they thought were hiding out in the bush. Culver put me and the children safely in a bedroom while he notified the police who arrested the ringleaders, thus preventing another clash.

There were many such incidents, but one more is worth

mentioning. Culver had just enjoyed a week without any major drama, and the day had started routinely. He and I were finishing breakfast when we heard banging and moaning at the back door. On opening the door, Culver saw one of his tappers slumped against the wall with a knife wound in his chest and what looked like a piece of lung hanging out. He also had a knife wound in his groin. He had struggled up the hill to get help from us. Culver called me for a second opinion. I was pretty used to these dramas by now and kept very calm. I looked closely and thought it was fat protruding from the wound. We bandaged the poor fellow and placed him gently into the ute. Culver phoned the police and then drove to the hospital. It turned out he had a collapsed lung, but he survived.

Culver had just returned home when another tapper rushed up to the house with an axe wound in his arm. This was the result of a domestic row. One fellow objected to the other talking to his wife, so he pulled out an axe. Others got involved trying to break up the scene. That meant another hospital visit and police report. Culver said he just thanked his lucky stars he had married a strong woman who could take all this in her stride.

These types of incidents didn't occur just on our plantation; all the other plantations had their troubles, too. Koitaki had an all-in brawl between three hundred members of the Chimbu tribe, and two hundred Goilalas. A Goilala had stolen a sweet potato from a Chimbu. Spears and clubs swung, battering the warriors, and a Chimbu died from a spear wound to the stomach.

Eilogo River flooding

Culver's Story

Culver on a boat to a local island near Port Moresby

The Papua Club
and
Planters' Association

Plantation Managers: Don Malcolm, Lisle Johnston, Brian Lukin, Culver Matley

In the early twentieth century the planters had already begun worrying that the limits of available PNG labour had been reached. They were pressing for three-year contracts and the admission of Asian workers. However, only short meetings were possible for the small, dispersed group of planters.

In 1913 the planters got together to form the Planters' Association. It initially represented the larger companies but grew to include most of the plantations within easy reach of Port Moresby. In the same year, the Papua Club was established by the same core of people including Tom Sefton and George Loudon, among others. It was like an English Gentlemen's Club. The purpose was to provide a friendly atmosphere for like-minded men, a refuge from the outside world, a place where they could eat, drink and talk in comfort and security. The club enabled planters to form partnerships with government administrators, businessmen, merchants, agents, and publicans. Sometimes they worked together to buy smaller plantations as they came up for sale.

Before the First World War, the Planters' Association held its board meetings at the Papua Club in Moresby, and afterwards they met in a private room in one of the better hotels. Several years went by without a meeting, and then a new Planters' Association was established in 1935 with a broader membership basis. Being a member of both the Papua Club and the Planters' Association was considered a high honour, and you needed an invitation to join. There was a strict dress code for both clubs. In the cooler weather, it was khaki gabardine trousers, brown shoes, a plain matching shirt and tie, and in hot weather, duck pants and a white, cotton twill shirt.

The Planters' Association was reformed in 1953 to address the planting communities' economic issues. For two years leading up to 1954, there was a severe financial crisis caused by poor varieties of rubber trees, high cost of production and transport, and the lack of an assured market in Australia. Even if the Commonwealth organised the planting of high-yielding trees, it would take ten years to reach the tapping stage. A few of the big plantations that were still making rubber profitably, weren't too keen to accept the added burden and cost of planting new areas, and the smaller planters couldn't afford to grow new areas. At that time, the rubber price barely met the cost of production—a perennial problem of agriculture.

Because Australian buyers had the choice of cheaper rubber from other countries, we were receiving a Grade 3 price for a product classed as Grade 1 and paying high freight costs on coastal shipping services. To cap it off, the Commonwealth Government had imposed a duty of tuppence per pound on PNG rubber imported into Australia. The cost of employing a rubber tapper was six shillings a day, compared with four shillings and sixpence in Malaya. Most plantation labour had to be recruited from remote areas and flown or shipped to the plantations. It took three to six months to train a tapper, and at the end of his two years he went back to his village, at the plantation's expense.

Generally, the PNG planter recruited and supervised his plantation labour and oversaw the clearing of the land. In Malaya, all these tasks were let out to Chinese contractors who also did the cleaning, weeding and rubber tapping. Tea, copra, and rubber producers from Sri Lanka to Singapore, had the benefit of the village community, and desertion was rare as labour was more settled. A village community also avoided the expense of recruiting and transporting labour. Unofficially, some administration officers favoured such a system in PNG.

The Commonwealth Government never allowed it. The main reason for their reluctance was the complexity of typical village life. Land ownership and land inheritance were complicated and intricate matters. The administration would have had to use a firm hand to introduce the system, which would have allowed some United Nations members to embarrass Australia. Russia, particularly, never missed a chance to criticise Australia's administration of PNG.

Also, shifting a village or group of villages to form a large village near a plantation would have involved land resumption, which the Administration wanted to avoid. Even though a local landowner who owned several hundred acres might only use his land for occasionally hunting wallabies, he was very reluctant to lose ownership of it.

We agreed with the Minister for Territories (Mr Paul Hasluck) that it was preferable to have normal village community life established on plantations instead of the recruitment of men only. Hasluck was appointed Minister for Territories in 1951 and given responsibility for PNG and the Northern Territory. He visited PNG regularly, and his view was the country should be gradually prepared for independence. Besides the importance of political development, Hasluck's priorities were education, health, law enforcement and employment, all of which were to be carried out by local officials. He also rejected any further attempts by Europeans to buy more land and insisted the Territory should raise its own revenue.

The United Nations was becoming increasingly critical of Australia's role in PNG. Australia's mandate from the UN required the country to be prepared for self-government. Hasluck also believed that, regarding local government, the traditional authority should be supported. In 1953, at the Commonwealth Government's invitation, a researcher from the Rubber Research Institute of Malaya surveyed the PNG rubber industry. His report was comprehensive and said the industry had good prospects, though he pointed out that the difficulties of training and retaining skilled native tappers were serious handicaps.

Another headache was Australian rubber companies' attitude toward our product. In 1952 the Australian companies told us they were overstocked and didn't require any more rubber. We faced a falling price and no market in Australia where the Government supposedly regarded the PNG industry as strategically important. For five months the planters received no cash returns, forcing small planters into bank overdrafts. Eventually, Mr Hasluck agreed to buy four hundred tons of Grade 1 rubber for the Federal stockpile. He released a similar amount of lower grade rubber from the stockpile, which Australian companies bought.

In 1953 two planters sent rubber samples to Germany for testing, which determined that these examples were Grade 1 quality. But the Australian buyers disagreed. Despite repeated requests to the Australian Government by the rubber growers, the government didn't take any firm steps to ensure a steady market in Australia. During the same year, representatives of the Planters' Association met with Commonwealth Government officials and a delegation of Australian rubber manufacturers. The Government failed to lift the duty on rubber imported into Australia, and we had no option but to accept the manufacturers' offer to buy first grade rubber for a Grade 3 price.

The month of May in PNG is supposed to be part of the dry season, but in May of 1954 it didn't stop raining. Because of the rain, Margaret and I spent a good deal of time inside upholstering chairs. We padded fibre and flock into hessian bags or pillows to make seats and nailed them down to the chair frames. Margaret sewed new seat covers. By the time we got to the dining chairs I suggested throwing them out and replacing them. At £14 a chair, Margaret persuaded me that sanding and staining would give them a new life for a few more seasons. For weeks it rained inches a day, and I thought it had something to do with the Americans dropping a hydrogen bomb in the Pacific back in early March. Equal to fifteen megatons of TNT, it was the largest United States nuclear test ever exploded. They didn't expect it to be that big and it gouged a crater half a mile wide, a hundred feet deep, and spewed several million tons of radioactive debris into the air.

Monthly board meetings of Eilogo Estates were usually rowdy. Even with the electric fans on full power, our shirts clung to our backs as we wiped sweat from our faces with handkerchiefs damp from the Moresby humidity. Repeating agenda items were the production costs, how to keep costs down, and securing an assured market for rubber. Our constant worry was how to make a profit with the duties we had to pay. Our Malayan competitors were trumping us time and time again with their cheap labour. Margaret even contributed her bit by sewing canvas bags for the tappers to collect the scrap rubber in. Every saving helped.

Another ongoing labour cost was keeping the jungle out of the rubber trees. The jungle was constantly trying to reclaim the plantations. We had teams of labourers whose only job was to cut down the vines, grass and weeds with long knives. It was time-consuming, hot, tedious work and an unpopular job. Over a few meetings and lots of discussion about different solutions to the problem, a unanimous vote agreed that cattle might be the answer. The idea was that the cattle would replace the men by keeping the grass and weeds down, and provide us with fresh meat, milk and cream. There had been a small number of cattle in PNG before the war, but combined with disease and their slaughter by both sides of the conflict, they were wiped out.

In February 1955 Ian Loudon chartered a Bristol Freighter from Australian National Airways to fly twenty-four head of Aberdeen Angus breeding stock from Rockhampton to Port Moresby, the first time an ANA plane had flown so far north. The cattle were then taken on to Eilogo by road. The same plane took 8,500 pounds of rubber back to Brisbane. It made national news in Australia.

Ian was the first to import cattle, but other planters quickly followed. Only a few weeks later, a large shipment of one thousand head of cattle was sent to a twenty thousand acre lease in the Goroka Valley, near Lae. The cattle travelled north in four stages. Everyone was convinced that a thriving cattle industry could be developed with the right breeds.

In November 1956, Prince Philip spent twelve days touring Papua New Guinea, Los Negros and the Northern Territory.

Government House in Port Moresby hosted a reception for him. When he heard the administration officials had cut down the number of guests to three hundred and excluded the local people, he said that all were to be let in. He then stood for three hours shaking hands with every island chief and every administration official and their wives.

The prince also had time for a plantation visit, and the Koitaki Club hosted a lunch in his honour. All the plantation managers and their wives were there, and the prince's charming personal magnetism put us all at ease. The Melbourne *Argus* reported: 'In the lavish (swimming pool, plush bar) Koitaki Club, overlooking the Kokoda Trail, the Duke strolled in after a heavy lunch with Mr. Colin Sefton, managing director of the Koitaki plantation, and, when asked to try his hand at clay pigeon shooting, patted his stomach and remarked with a grin: 'I'm afraid I'd fall over backwards!'

HRH The Duke of Edinburgh at the Koitaki Club

Back
to
Canada

Margaret and Beth at Mororo

The year 1957 was a memorable one for many reasons. I had planned to take Margaret to meet my folks in Canada that year. Profits from the rubber were good for once, and I could afford the trip after a twenty-two-year absence.

Mororo, which I was managing, was doing well. It was half the size of Eilogo, but still made £22,000 to Eilogo's £53,000, with which everyone was pleased. I owned a quarter interest and was very satisfied that both my hard work and my investment were finally paying off.

After lots of discussions, Margaret finally decided she couldn't go to Canada. When our third child, Anthea, was born in Moresby in March, the timing couldn't have been worse. Taking a baby to Canada was out of the question, and Margaret felt she couldn't leave her behind for two months. Beth and Christina were older and could have been left with Margaret's folks, but not the baby. It was such a disappointment for both of us. My mother was eighty-one and my father seventy-six, and I wasn't expecting to make the trip again. Margaret decided that she and the children would stay in Horsham.

I flew with the family to Sydney, then we travelled by train to Melbourne and on to Horsham, where a local journalist heard of our visit to Horsham and asked for an interview. I agreed but regretted it afterwards. He was aggressive in his interview and suggested that my family and I lived a life of privilege in a tropical paradise with cheap labour, house servants and extensive holidays.

I tried to explain that it took two years of constant work to earn a two-month holiday. Those two months were usually spent in Victoria, with Margaret's family in Horsham or at the beach at Anglesea, our favourite holiday place, and not in a five-star resort. Wages were higher in PNG, compared with Australia, but so was the cost of living. The shipping and freight costs to get food staples made goods expensive. The high cost of commodities such as tea, rice and flour were due to the lack of subsidies that the mainland received. I told him that grumbling Victorians should go to PNG and try to live as cheaply as they did in Victoria.

When the journalist asked how easy it would be to get work there, and that the whole setup sounded ideal, I laughed. I pointed out that work was plentiful alright, but accommodation was virtually impossible. Most of the bigger offices, banks and companies had their own hostels for their employees. He also asked if Margaret was lonely, being the only white woman on the plantation. I explained she was a member of a very active branch of the CWA at Sogeri and made regular trips to Port Moresby where she also had friends.

After that interview I couldn't wait to board the train to Melbourne and fly to Sydney and on to Canada.

I boarded the Qantas Super Constellation airliner, nicknamed 'Connie', in Sydney. The 59 other passengers were dressed for the occasion. The men wore three-piece suits, and the women smart dresses and high heels, as we climbed aboard via an outside staircase. It was a world-class aeroplane for its time, a high-speed, four-engine, propeller-driven aircraft. It had a distinctive triple-tail design and a graceful, dolphin-shaped fuselage. With its pressurised cabin we could climb above 12,500 feet, which took us out of the airsickness zone and above any turbulent weather.

It also had air-conditioning and reclining seats, which meant I could stretch out in comfort. Air hostesses moved through wide aisles ensuring the champagne and brandy flowed freely. A cocktail lounge provided canapés and drinks for those passengers who wanted to socialise. It didn't take long for the aircraft to fill with cigar and cigarette smoke. The dining room buffet tables usually had lobster and beef, and meals were served with linen napkins. The meals usually lasted three hours and helped to pass the time

After fuel stops at Nadi in Fiji, and Canton Island in Kiribati, the plane flew to Hawaii for an overnight stay. Passengers were accommodated at The Royal Hawaiian beachside resort on Waikiki Beach. It was a luxurious travel resort built on fifteen acres of beach frontage. Sitting at one of the restaurant's outside tables, I could see the beachfront lagoon. Sailors in full uniform mingled with people dressed in beachwear on the white sandy beach. In the distance, the

Qantas Connie aeroplane prior to departure,
San Francisco, 1957

surf pounded the coral reef that protected the lagoon's calm water. I watched the setting sun illuminating Diamond Head's ridgeline, shaped like a tuna's dorsal fin, and wished Margaret was with me. Just before an orange sunset slipped below the horizon, I took a photo with palm fronds bending over the calm water, to show her.

The Connie made a stopover in San Francisco the next day, and then we flew on to Vancouver. I had sent money to my parents so they could fly from Saskatoon to meet me. When I finally stepped onto Canadian soil at Vancouver Airport and cleared customs, I saw my folks and sister Mary waving enthusiastically at the gate.

Father looked much older than his 76 years: pale, and too thin. He still had his ramrod-straight back and shook my hand warmly. Mother couldn't keep the smile off her face as I kissed her cheek. My brother Arthur couldn't make it because of the combination of a young family and work. When I heard he would meet me in Saskatoon, I thought of the young family I had left behind to travel halfway around the world, on what was likely to be my only visit to see family, but I quickly shook off the sadness.

We spent a couple of days sightseeing around that beautiful harbour before we were due to fly to Saskatoon. A highlight was a ferry trip to Vancouver Island to visit the Butchart Gardens, a fifty-five acre oasis of blooms and a garden-lover's delight. My mother loved them, and I took many photos for Margaret.

I barely recognised Saskatoon as the small rural town I had left twenty-two years previously. It was now a thriving city with more than 100,000 people, with shopping centres and housing estates, one of which my folks had moved into. I made their home my base while I made brief visits to revisit favourite places and to catch up with old friends and family. Mary and I travelled the 140 miles by train to Regina, where she lived and taught at Peart Elementary School. It was a brief visit, as my time was limited, and I had a lot of country to travel to get what I wanted done.

I went on alone to Ottawa to see my favourite brother, Francis. Greying, quiet, and retired now, he still had the energy to show me the city and Parliament House where he had worked in the library as a cataloguer. My two months flew by, and the time came to farewell my folks. It was painful, and I felt the beginnings of tears as I turned to wave. It turned out, this would be my last goodbye to my parents.

Francis, Mary, Arthur (Jack), Martha and Culver Matley
1957

Eilogo Plantation
1957–1966

Creek crossing, Sogeri district

The Round Australia Redex Trial started in 1953 and was considered the most challenging off-road car race in Australia. To survive the distance between checkpoints, drivers had to carry extra fuel, sand mats, shovels, picks and enough water and food to sustain them. Most of Australia's roads back then were in very poor condition or were mere dirt tracks. The Trial, which involved both amateur and professional entrants driving average, unmodified cars across rough terrain, generated enormous interest. It was an unheard-of idea, then, to drive the length and breadth of Australia in an ordinary car.

Ken Tubman, a 27-year-old chemist from Maitland in NSW, and his mate John Marshall, won the inaugural 6,500 mile race in a Peugeot 203. They collected gifts, and prize money of £1,500. They competed against Holdens, Humbers, Chryslers and Plymouths. The Peugeot was a rugged French car that had first appeared in 1948. In that same year, two Frenchmen drove a 203 from Cape Town to Paris, around 9,300 miles, in just seventeen days.

Ernie Kriewaldt, a motorsports enthusiast who ran a furniture store in Port Moresby, decided he would like to participate. He began to prepare a 203 for the 1955 Redex Trial. He approached every businessman in Port Moresby for sponsorship, and Ian Loudon was impressed by his pitch.

'What makes it the right car?' he asked Ernie.

'It's got a small engine, with low fuel consumption, but it's rugged and can easily be fixed on the road.'

Ernie got his funding and entered the trial. The conditions were so rough only about half the cars finished the race. Ernie failed to finish. He hit a tree near Innisfail and wrecked the car.

Ernie's accident didn't deter Ian, who ordered a Peugeot as his personal transport. In 1957, Ian was thirty-seven years old, managing and living on the Eilogo plantation with his wife and two young boys. His parents, George and Peg, had retired to Sydney. One late night in November, I received a phone call that changed our lives. Ian had been involved in an accident.

There was a low-level bridge on the road to Eilogo. As I've mentioned previously, pre-war it was wooden and had been swept away in a flood. Early in the war, engineers rebuilt it as a low-level steel and concrete structure. There had already been many vehicle accidents on this bridge, as it was approached by a twisting downhill road, and it had low sidewalls.

Ian was returning from Moresby in his Peugeot, and a thick fog blanketed the bridge. His car hit the left bank then swung off the road, over the bridge and into the river, landing upside down in less than two feet of water. Ian, knocked unconscious, drowned. He would have survived if someone had been there to lift his head out of the water.

More than three hundred people from all over the Territory attended his funeral in Port Moresby, where he was buried. One group even pioneered a new road through the forest to get to the funeral. Senior Administration officers and business leaders described him as the most popular man in the Territory. Ian's wife, Margaret, donated his piano to the Papua Club and as soon as probate was granted, she and the children left for Sydney.

It was a blow to the Territory, but a devastating loss to our district, one from which we never fully recovered. For someone who had survived so many near misses during the war to die in those circumstances, was beyond comprehension. Ian's death seemed to emphasise the futility of what we were doing on those plantations.

After the funeral, Mr and Mrs Loudon asked me to take over Ian's role, as a trial manager, and to move my family into the Eilogo homestead. I found my new role busy and demanding, what with the new workers to train, organising the various workgroups, maintaining machinery and ensuring that health and hygiene requirements were strictly met. However, without Ian's vibrant personality to keep our spirits up, a sense of sadness seemed to permeate everything.

Added to this loss was the sense our futures were becoming less certain for political reasons. By 1957, there was growing international pressure for Australia to grant independence to PNG, though the Australian Prime Minister Robert Menzies and his government strongly resisted this pressure. Indonesia was continuing its claim to West Papua, which was then called West Irian.

There were calls for a Dutch-Australian military alliance to keep Indonesia out of West Irian, but there was also the fear that this might end in a war with the eighty million Indonesians and many millions of other Asians who supported Indonesia's claim. We certainly feared that this could overwhelm us in PNG. The uncertainty continued for a couple of years, with the United Nations demanding Australia set a timetable for independence. Indonesia nationalised all Dutch assets, and the Dutch responded by proposing that Papua New Guinea and West Irian merge as an independent Melanesian state.

In October 1959, I chaired an Extraordinary General Meeting of Catalina Estate Limited to discuss ways of cutting costs. We passed a resolution to liquidate the company voluntarily, and John Lukin was appointed liquidator. The estate became amalgamated with Eilogo and Mororo, and I became responsible for the overall administration of the three plantations.

Disputes between tribes were becoming more common and required a lot of diplomacy and tact to prevent them escalating. Paybacks and individual fights occurred, but there was often a warning that problems were brewing. I had to be aware of my own, and my family's safety, as there was no support or help in an emergency. I kept a revolver under my pillow at night, but never carried it. The hunting rifles were kept clean, but locked in a gun safe.

One example of my anxiety over safety occurred one night when I was leaving the bathroom. Anthea's bedroom was on the other side of the centre garden, away from the rest of the family. She had to cross the garden via a little path to visit the bathroom. This night she reached the bathroom just as I was coming out. She crept up behind me and said, 'Boo!' I swung around to strike whoever I thought was going to attack me. Fortunately, she was short, and my arm passed just over her head. I leant down, shaking and thinking of what could have happened if she had been taller.

April 1959 heralded the arrival of our fourth child, John. I was nursing him in the maternity ward in the Port Moresby hospital and watching Margaret brushing her thick hair.

Suddenly she dropped the brush and leaned in closer to the mirror.

'I've found my first grey hairs! About six! Come and have a look.'

'I don't think they'll be the last he'll give you either!' was my reply.

Eileen Johnston was minding eleven-year-old Beth, eight-year-old Christina and two-year-old Anthea until we returned on Anzac Day, a week later. They all rushed out to the car to greet us. Once everyone was inside the house and settled, Christina, with grand ceremony, presented Margaret with a gift from us all—an electric sewing machine. I hadn't been deaf to the number of hints I had received during the year, the numerous mentions of the wonders that this automatic Singer machine could do. Margaret had even left her women's magazines lying around, the pages open to the advertisements promising how much time its automated features could save the housewife.

Over the next few days, the constant stream of visitors dropping by with cards, gifts and messages of congratulations had us wondering about all the fuss. As Margaret pointed out, 'By the time you get to the fourth, it's not headline news anymore.' We put the visitors' interest down to the baby being a boy.

There were often crises with the children, and we had to cope with them because of our isolation. We had nurse girls to keep an eye on them, but they still managed to get into strife. One case involved some white-spotted, green-leafed shrubs Margaret had planted that were thriving as if no bug would touch them. Christina had broken a leaf off this plant and put it in her mouth. Well! We heard her screams from the garden. Rushing down to her, we managed to calm her enough to show us what she'd done.

I touched my mouth with the stalk, and it burned, so Christina couldn't have swallowed any as the reaction was too sudden. We waited it out. Before it stopped, two hours with saliva pouring from her mouth was hard to watch. The next day, both she and I had blisters in our mouths. Margaret instructed the gardener to dig up all the plants and burn them.

Another time I was at the bakery giving instructions and checking on the trade store supplies when the phone rang twice on the party line. It was Margaret and urgent.

'Anthea's swallowed some furniture polish!'

It only took a few minutes to run down to the house. When I arrived, I could smell the chemical Anthea had vomited but it didn't look like much, probably no more than a mouthful. We gave her a drink of milk which soon settled her down. The previous week it was kerosene, so we tried to make sure none of these chemicals were left lying around, but accidents still happened.

Apart from our weekend socialising, we spent most of our time on our own, but there was no shortage of books and music. With the spasmodic reception, the radio was only turned on once a day for some news from the Australian Broadcasting Commission (ABC). The record player was in high demand, with records ranging from jazz and country to children's stories. A small guest house near the primary residence was known as the Waldorf. If a manager had to be away from home overnight, his wife and children would stay there. It also accommodated occasional visitors, especially ones escaping a Victorian winter.

There was some occasional relief from the isolation. Allied troops had used a building overlooking Rouna Falls as a canteen during the war. Afterwards it became a teashop and then the proprietor, Dorothea Troeth, obtained a liquor license and turned it into a popular hotel. Everyone called her Woody and the hotel was known as Woody's Pub. Woody and her hotel were very popular with everyone in the district. At one stage she even had a private zoo. Large possums, wallabies, crocodiles, birds of paradise, pythons and tree-climbing kangaroos kept children entertained while the adults knocked back their beers.

Occasionally, I rented a movie for the staff to watch on Saturday night in an open-sided, wooden-beamed, thatched-

Anthea and nurse girl holding John in the garden, Eilogo

roof hall. There was usually a tropical downpour during these screenings, but that didn't deter the eager patrons. They clapped, cheered, pointed and shouted at the unfolding drama on the screen, with rolls of thunder overhead.

Our children grew up playing with the children of our staff, who lived on the premises. They learned Motu from their nannies before they learned English. On non-school days, our son John often disappeared with the cook's sons. They'd each take a loaf of bread and a water bottle and wander for miles, sometimes calling into a local garden for sugarcane or pineapple, or whatever they could scrounge. The cook's boys had a good bush sense and never got lost.

As the children grew older, Margaret wished we lived closer to civilisation and good schools, things most people in Australia took for granted. Beth, who had some special needs, did best with family around her. Being a family type, Margaret grew less and less keen on leaving her parents, siblings, nieces and nephews after our leave visits to Horsham. Me, not so much. I had grown to love PNG and its people. Even though I wasn't much of a 'man's man', I had made some good friends and couldn't think of another life I could lead and enjoy as much.

By 1960 the white residents of PNG were beginning to question their future. The Australian Minister for Territories, Paul Hasluck, had said that independence would not happen for thirty years, but we didn't believe him. The Russians and their allies repeatedly criticised Australia for the mismanagement of PNG. In early 1961, the Indonesian Defence Minister, Nasution, went to Moscow instead of Canberra, to emphasise

Australia's isolation on the West Irian question. Premier Khrushchev spoke in support of Indonesia's struggle against the Imperialists. Russia's demand for immediate independence of New Guinea in the UN Trusteeship Council was lost by only one vote.

Then, in September 1961, the year our fifth child, Sonya, was born, Indonesia landed armed troops in West Irian.

In August 1962, Operation Spectrum was put in place by the Dutch to evacuate five thousand women and children to West Irian. It was not hard to imagine something similar happening to us in a few years' time in PNG. Indonesia gained control of West Irian in May 1963, and the press reported that President Soekarno had his eye on the rest of Papua New Guinea and Portuguese Timor. We felt the family's future was uncertain, due to the Indonesian threat and the declining rubber industry.

A new House of Assembly, a truly representative parliament, was opened in Port Moresby in 1964. Locals began to replace expatriate public servants. There was a debate about whether English or pidgin should be the national language, with English eventually chosen. A large migration began from the highland villages to shanties on the outskirts of the towns.

Changes at home were making life more difficult. Gambling had become such a problem that the Parliament of New Guinea, in which various village members had a majority, passed a law that made card playing a crime. The European community who, having no television, spent much time playing bridge and other card games, was dismayed.

One day in 1965 Margaret was reading the newspaper when she threw it down saying, 'Oh no, this is the last straw!'

I scanned the offending article, reading:

... it is an offence to play any sort of cards in a private home unless the cards have been hired or borrowed from a licensed card playing premises and returned as soon as possible. Bridge players who play with their own cards in their own homes, for example, are liable to three months' gaol

Margaret knew the local people couldn't stop gambling. It was a huge problem. People were losing too much money. Women and children were usually left with nothing after the men lost all their wages on gambling. Then Margaret spoke the words I had been both dreading and expecting: 'Maybe it's time to think whether we have a future here after all.'

As if he had heard her, the Deputy Leader of the Federal Opposition, Gough Whitlam, said that Australia should be out of New Guinea by 1970. This statement was countered by the Minister for Territories, Mr Barnes, who said:

The moment Papua New Guinea becomes independent, she will be subject to all kinds of external pressure. It is obvious, for instance, that Indonesia will try to extend her influence over the Eastern part of the island. It is a safe bet that Communist China will wish to build a large embassy in Port Moresby from which she can direct propaganda and subversion. Other countries, too, will be anxious to seek advantages in trade.

At this time Australia was closely watching events in Northern Rhodesia, where the Smith government had unilaterally declared independence from Britain. The possible parallels with PNG were alarming. At the end of 1966 the UN voted fifty-nine to fifteen for Australia to set an early date for PNG's independence.

By the mid to late 1960s, it was becoming harder to find suitable workers willing to do what they now considered was menial work. This was due in part to the higher level of education. Plantation work was done mainly by men, but they weren't too keen on letting their womenfolk do the work either. Women were still expected to tend the village gardens and mind the children.

I wrote to my father-in-law who owned a real estate business in Horsham, and he promised me a job. That cemented our decision to leave PNG and resettle in Australia.

Margaret on Moresby wharf, 1962

Life at Eilogo

Matley home, Eilogo

Margaret in the centre garden at Eilogo

In the garden at Eilogo
(Culver with John, Christina and Anthea)

Gardener at Eilogo

Swimming pool at Koitaki Club

Waiting for the plane to travel south to Australia,
Port Moresby, 1960

Anthea as the Yellow Rose of Texas at fancy dress party,
Sogeri, 1960

Changes Afoot:
Eilogo 1967

Rubber plant at Eilogo

Latex vats at Eilogo

When George Loudon died in 1964, his wife, Peg, who was living in Sydney, became my employer. In 1967, I wrote to her about the difficult decision Margaret and I had made. We had been talking about it to each other for about a year, and with the other plantation managers, and with Mrs Loudon, so my letter came as no surprise to her.

I sent the following letter to Peg:

27th April 1967

Dear Mrs Loudon,

This is the most difficult and painful letter to write but I must tell you I will not be able to return to Eilogo after the completion of my present term in December. This will not come as a surprise to you as I told Bud last June that I would have to make a decision about my future.

My main reason for leaving here is the situation with my family. Beth is now 19 years old and becoming increasingly difficult to manage in this isolated way of life. She needs family life but more freedom than we can give her here. As for the other children, we have one at boarding school and three more facing secondary school. This in itself is impossible for me financially but could be overcome except for the other factors in the situation, the condition of Beth, declining fortunes of the rubber industry and the uncertainty of the future as the Territory moves towards independence.

Please don't think that this decision has been made without a lot of thought. One does not give up lightly, a position in which a whole working life has been spent and attempt to start a new life in new surroundings. I am 53 and have no qualifications except for the job I have been doing, very little money, but a real desire to do the best I can for my family while there is still time.

I have been treated generously here and I thank you for all the consideration that has been given to me over the years. I deeply regret leaving Eilogo when the Company is going through difficult times but feel that with the new areas coming into production that better times lie ahead. I do not want to cut all connections with Eilogo and hope that I may remain as a director. I think that my experience could be of some value to the Company still.

Mrs Loudon wrote back:

6th May 1967

Dear Culver

Your letter has arrived and has saddened me. I was expecting to hear from you, but even though it was not actually a surprise, it was still a great blow. I can't imagine Eilogo without you.

I fully understand your reasons for leaving, and feel you are doing the right thing under the circumstances, much as I regret it. It was a big decision for you to make and I admire you for making the only one possible.

The family will benefit from the move. You will feel you have accepted the challenge and I hope the future will be kind to you. You deserve it.

I'd hoped against hope that Eilogo would sell and everyone receive sufficient to plan a new life. Though that letter was rather a blow, at least we now have a definite decision. We will certainly need you as a director, Culver. Your experience and knowledge will be of great value to us.

My love to Margaret and to yourself.
Very Sincerely
Peggy Loudon

I resigned as manager in May 1967, and John Lukin took up the position and moved into the Eilogo house. I was leaving a land I loved. From the age of twenty-one until fifty-three this had been my home. I'd started my career, met my wife and had my children in that beautiful country. You can't just walk away from all that, at least not lightly. .

Rubber processing, Eilogo

Anthea's Memories of Leaving Eilogo and PNG

The weeks before our final departure were hectic. Tea chests sat everywhere half-filled with paper-wrapped fragile goods—glasses, plates, cups, ornaments, everything that made a house a home. The rhythm of the house, the daily routine, the general certainty of the order of the day turned into organised chaos. My mother gave final instructions to the house servants in shrill tones—the tension in my father's shoulders drove me outside.

We kids filed out, our eyes downcast, and piled into the waiting white Holden. No one spoke. Mum sat in the passenger seat, one hand clutching her handbag, the other holding a damp handkerchief to wet eyes. Her shoulders were rigid, her mouth tight. Father was the last to get into the car. He sat for a moment, not turning around, then turned on the ignition. We heard a deafening roar as two hundred men lifted their spears and shouted. Father turned off the engine.

'I'll have to go back and say one last goodbye.' Not looking at Mum, who was staring straight ahead, he got out of the car.

We watched through the back window as Dad walked along the long colourful line of men, shaking each hand, touching an occasional shoulder, until he reached the head man. They spoke for a long time, holding each other by the wrists, seeming not to want to let go. Eventually, Father returned to the car, his head down.

'They don't want me to leave,' he said, starting the car. We knelt on the seat, looking out the back window at the crowd. Most were sitting on the ground, others paced up and down. We turned the first corner, and they were lost to view.

Each member of the family struggled, in their own way, to adjust to living in the rural community of Horsham. It took some time to settle into a new rhythm of life. To ease the transition, Dad would clean our school shoes and bring tea and toast to our rooms for our breakfast. Mum taught us how to make our beds and change the sheets.

School was problematic. Though we lived within walking distance of the primary school, for a time Sonya had to be driven to school and dragged from the car, crying and screaming into the schoolyard.

I walked into my first class to hear all the children chanting numbers. I didn't know what they were doing but was soon told they were chanting the times tables, something I hadn't heard of before. In my free time I would try to hide from the other children, from their curiosity. They would find me, and the inevitable questions would come.

'Where are you from?'

'Papua New Guinea,' I'd reply.

'Why haven't you got black, frizzy hair?'

High school was a blessing and a fresh start for us, and we

made many friends there. We all, eventually, found our place in our new home, Australia.

Dad, having no formal qualifications, was unable to obtain employment. His skills of recruiting staff, managing property, finances and a labour force were of no interest to Australian employers. His promised job in real estate didn't eventuate. Instead, it went to his brother-in-law who had convinced Mum's father that his need for employment was greater. Dad purchased two investment properties and received a small income from renting them out. He spent his time maintaining them, helping Mum in the house, and establishing a useful workshop where he could fix anything.

To try to give the other children some normality during their high school years, Beth was sent to board with a family in Bowral, New South Wales. Mum and Dad initially got by on savings and investments which gradually dwindled over the years. After they sold their house in Horsham and moved to Portarlington, they lived on age pensions.

Port Moresby
2018

Pacific Ocean, Port Moresby, PNG, 2018

At the beginning of September 2018, long after my parents had passed away, I said to my husband, Peter, 'I want to go back to New Guinea. Do you think we can do it? Will you help me?' He readily agreed, and a couple of weeks later, we were on a flight to Port Moresby. We had no plan other than booking a room at the Grand Papua Hotel. We'd agreed to see how things were when we landed and allowed ourselves five days for the trip.

I popped the pressure in my ears as the plane descended to Jackson Airport, Port Moresby. A modern-looking airport terminal had replaced the tin shed I remembered from five decades earlier. Jackson Airport is at 7 Mile, eleven kilometres from the city. We were the only white people among the passengers, who, I assumed, were either travelling home from shopping or working in Brisbane. Everyone was in a good mood with lots of laughter and chatter, and although we exchanged smiles with several of our fellow passengers, we didn't speak with them.

After disembarking and reaching border control, I handed over my documents to the serious-looking young woman with her long black hair pulled tightly into a neat bun on top of her head. She wore a pale blue, open-necked shirt with a colourful emblem on the sleeve and a matching dark blue skirt.

'What is the purpose of your visit?' she asked, taking my passport and papers and closely studying my identification details.

'It says here you were born in Port Moresby.' She looked up at me, her eyes widening.

'Yes! I was born here. I've come back for a visit,' I replied with a smile.

She laughed, shaking her head. 'You were born here! Welcome home.' She lifted her arm high, stamped our visas with a flourish and waved us through, still smiling. I nearly cried at the warmth of her welcome and felt I had made the right decision to embark on this sentimental journey.

We moved outside the airport to the pick-up area. The hotel had promised to send a car to meet us. As soon as we stepped out of the air-conditioned building we started to perspire. The air was hot and humid, with a blustery wind raising dust and rubbish in little eddies in the corners of the buildings. It seemed to change direction continually, and we couldn't find any shelter. Our shirts clung to our bodies, and grit stuck to our sweaty faces. September is a warm, dry month in PNG but still humid. A shower and changing from travelling clothes were a priority.

The airport was quiet. Below the 'Welcome to Papua New Guinea' sign was a large warning, 'No betel nut chewing. No smoking'. Our fellow passengers quickly disappeared out the front doors to waiting vehicles or to continue their journeys on foot. Soon, we were the only ones waiting. After an hour, we phoned the hotel and eventually a large van arrived to collect us. We were the only passengers.

The slow drive through the city's outskirts gave us plenty of time to take in the suburbs bustling with people, mainly men. Most had beards and either squatted or stood in small groups outside graffitied buildings. Dressed in shorts and T-shirts with fading slogans, they spat, smoked, and argued. According to our driver, the piles of rubbish littering the sides of the road were due to an ongoing garbage strike. In contrast, the central city area looked like any modern city, with high-rise buildings, and lots of traffic (both vehicular and foot) as people went about their business.

The driver explained it was a month before the Asia-Pacific Economic Cooperation (APEC) forum, and the PNG government wanted the city cleaned up before the international visitors arrived. Betel nut chewing, popular and rampant throughout the country, was banned. When mixed in the mouth with mustard and lime, chewed betel nut produces a red liquid. When it's spat onto the concrete pavements and curbs, removing the stains it makes is very difficult.

At the Grand Papua Hotel, we asked a young man at the reception if he could arrange a four-wheel-drive vehicle and

Buildings of Port Moresby, 2018

security driver to take us into the mountains. He looked inexperienced and flustered, so he called another young man over who asked us what we wanted. He too looked unsure and called a third person, a young woman, who was more fluent in English. They either didn't understand what we were asking for, or genuinely couldn't help, because they were vague in their answers, looking at each other and shaking their heads. We decided not to pursue it and went to our room.

With some effort, we got onto the internet and tracked down an Australian-run security firm. The process took most of our first day before we found the necessary vehicle and driver. The difficulty was specifically requesting a four-wheel-drive vehicle. City cars were plentiful but not what we needed. My brother had walked the Kokoda Track a few years before and had tried to visit the plantation we grew up on but was unable to due to the road's poor condition. He said we would need a four-wheel-drive vehicle to tackle it. We finally arranged a vehicle and driver to take us inland in three days' time.

The next morning we thought we would do some sight-seeing.

'Is it safe to walk the streets?' I asked the desk staff.

'Oh yes. Safe,' they said, nodding.

We headed down to Ela Beach, about four hundred metres from the hotel. I had great memories of family outings here under the shade of coconut trees, playing in the sand, and paddling in the warm ocean, the laughter and shrieks as a thronging mixture of European and local people picnicked and swam together. We crossed a busy four-lane highway, and we had to use the pedestrian crossing button to cross the road.

From the highway we could see the beach. It was a sad sight. All the trees and vegetation had been removed, and it looked denuded and lifeless, with yellow plastic barriers roping off the sand. There wasn't a soul on the beach, or in the water. A fancy new conference centre had been built on the foreshore in anticipation of the expected foreign visitors, and the government didn't want anyone messing up the beach.

We continued our walk along the footpath, following the shoreline in search of a café we'd read in a hotel brochure was worth visiting. The hot wind blew relentlessly. The occasional vehicle making its way down Bramell Street slowed down, the occupants staring at us—probably wondering why on earth we would choose to walk around in this uncomfortable heat and wind.

We approached the busy waterfront which hugs the south side of the harbour and where lots of road construction was in progress. We walked and walked but couldn't find the café. Eventually, we passed the busy port and headed into a deserted area. We stopped to look at the map, and a police car pulled up. The officer was a policewoman from New Zealand, sent to help with law and order during the APEC summit.

'Can I help you two?' she asked. 'I saw you were looking a bit lost, and you don't want to do that here, it's too dangerous. Hop in, and I'll take you where you want to go.'

She knew of the café we were looking for and drove us down to the wharf where it was located. We had to go through a security gate to get into the wharf area. Before driving off, she warned, 'Keep to the main thoroughfares.'

There was another round of security to get past before we came to the restaurant area.

The Duffy Café, built right beside the water, was on a wooden deck overlooking the harbour. The day was hot, but large umbrellas sheltered us with ample shade. A cool breeze blew straight off the water as we sipped fresh coconut water served in a half coconut shell, its papery husk, soft and brown. With a sense of peace from the hot and bustling city streets, we gazed at the green hills surrounding the deep blue water of the harbour.

It was a different harbour from the one I remembered. My vague recollections were of crowds of people, blasting horns of ships, shouting and laughter. It was alive! Now, no one could get down here without having to go through tight security. It was quiet and hushed. Even the seagulls maintained a wary distance and kept their beaks closed.

The café was popular, not crowded, but people came and went. I assumed they were from the nearby office buildings, as they came with laptops and mobile phones. Some were having Zoom meetings, and others were meeting face-to-face with notepads and pens, taking notes as they talked. Everyone spoke quietly, even in their meetings. This added to the tranquil feeling of the café and general harbourside.

The harbour view was familiar, even though when we lived in PNG it was usually glimpsed from the car window as we drove into town for shopping, or on a Sunday drive to a beach nearby. But we could always hear the sounds of the busy harbour.

We ordered coffee to prolong our visit. Duffy's only serves coffee grown locally in the highlands and so delicious and full of flavour we had to order another. Eventually, we had to leave. Our waiter was Italian and too busy to chat but told us to stick to the main road when we returned to the hotel. All the shops along the road had security guards, he assured us. We walked through a shopping centre which led to an underpass. A middle-aged woman was rushing past when she suddenly stopped and asked my name.

'I'm Heather,' she smiled, clutching my hand with hers. 'Welcome, welcome.'

I thanked her with a smile, and she ran on. We continued, stopping at an ATM with a guard stationed by it. A local woman was using it when she turned and saw us. Her face lit up.

'What's your name? I'm Judith.'

There were no other Westerners on the streets, so we attracted a lot of attention. People either stared at us or waved.

During dinner that evening, the hotel manager, an Australian, approached us. Average height, with grey curly hair and wearing a grey uniform of short-sleeved shirt and skirt, she wanted to know if we enjoyed our meal and whether the wait staff had been helpful. Her smile was strained as if it was something she wasn't used to. The staff kept well clear, I noticed. We assured her we were very satisfied with our wait staff, which seemed to relax her, as her shoulders dropped a little and she became almost chatty.

'What brings you to Port Moresby?'

'A holiday,' we replied.

She gave a humourless laugh, more a snort really and looked incredulous.

'No one comes here for a holiday. There's nothing to do.'

She laughed. 'My contract finishes at the end of the year, and I'm looking forward to going back to Australia.'

She was right about there being nothing for visitors to do. There were no boats to hire for a day trip to any of the shimmering, inviting nearby islands, the museum was closed for an upgrade, and it seemed there were no public parks nearby.

Unbeknownst to us, one of the hotel desk staff arranged for a car and driver to take us for a tour of the city the next day. Ben was short, looked about forty, with thick wiry hair, and he was full of energy and enthusiasm. He had stuck the Mount Hagen flag prominently on the bonnet of his dilapidated Toyota to show how proud he was of his region. Ben showed us the local markets, downtown city, and suburban shopping centres, all of which were doing a brisk trade. He pointed out all the high-security fences surrounding almost every building in the downtown area. They were mainly hotels, banks, businesses and offices. He then drove us to the suburb of Waigani to visit Parliament House, adjacent to the Supreme Court Buildings. It's a stunningly beautiful building with its modern architecture blended with ancient tribal designs. A four-lane, one-kilometre-long bitumen road, for use by government officials only, led to the entrance. Ben laughed as we shook our heads. 'This Government is pretending we're a first world country when, really, we are a third world country.'

We felt safe and comfortable in Moresby, just as I had done, when growing up, but we didn't risk going out after dark. Each evening we sat on the hotel's balcony, looking out over the harbour and the street below. We watched the sun setting behind the hills and mountains, lighting the edges of rain-promising clouds. The lights from the surrounding buildings and streetlights splashed their reflections on the calm waters of the harbour.

On our fourth day, our driver arrived at the hotel with a flash four-wheel-drive, the type used in Australian cities by parents ferrying their children to school. Not quite the robust vehicle I knew we would need to tackle the often washed-out roads, but it would have to do. We were running out of time.

'I'm Graham,' announced the 183-centimetre tall, broad-shouldered, bald man, holding out his hand and smiling widely. His dark skin gleamed against his black suit, white shirt and company tie. I didn't doubt the heavy jacket, worn in the heat, also concealed a small handgun. We shook hands, introduced ourselves, and he invited me to sit in the front of the air-conditioned vehicle to get the best view. Graham was interested in why we had come to Port Moresby and keen to see a part of his country he hadn't yet visited. We drove through an ever-expanding city. The suburbs were now overtaking what was once the countryside.

The Sogeri road begins at the 9 Mile settlement, north-east of Moresby along the Hubert Murray Highway, and accessed by taking a right-hand exit at the large roundabout. So much had changed. Major settlements bordered the road and the streets teemed with people. This is the road that, in the Second World War, soldiers from engineering, ordnance, signals, survey, transport, medical and convalescent units, travelled on and camped beside. Around three kilometres furhter on, we could see in the distance the Hombrom and Wariarata bluffs of the Owen Stanley Range.

The Bomana War Cemetery was close by, and we took a short break to wander through this beautiful and immaculately kept cemetery. Many of those who died fighting in Papua and Bougainville were brought here to be buried. Local staff maintain it and the garden, which is financed by the Office of Australian War Graves in Canberra. We had a contemplative walk through simple wrought-iron gates onto a grass forecourt and climbed a short flight of steps to the Stone of Remembrance, an altar of pink stone. Just beyond, on gentle slopes, were the graves, marked by rows and rows of white marble headstones that stand stark against the bright green of the lawns. In the centre, the focus of the whole cemetery, stood the Cross of Sacrifice, made from the same stone as the altar. We were the only ones visiting that morning. The tropical plants and magnificent rainforest trees added to the peaceful setting.

We continued our drive on a well-made bitumen road through a mixture of scrubby-looking cycads, eucalypts and tall, blade-like grasses. Though now sealed, it was still the narrow road I remembered. A red dirt road back then, it was regularly washed out during torrential monsoon rains.

The road from Bomana to Rouna Falls was dubbed the Snake Road by Second World War soldiers, as it has a few steep S-bends. We travelled along the Laloki Valley, which rises and narrows at its peak, ending at the base of the Rouna Falls where two familiar massive bluffs dominate—Hombrom and Wariarata. One is a spur, and the other is the point where the thirty-kilometre-long Astrolabe Range terminates. As we climbed the valley, the trees increased in size, and pockets of rainforest trees appeared dominated by tall green grass. Nearing the first of the S-bends, the Devil's Elbow, I saw the familiar large, black volcanic boulders scattered throughout the landscape. The road twisted around the mountainside until we reached the falls.

Graham parked the car, and we took a two-minute walk down to the lookout to view the falls cascading to a rock pool below. From here we could see tropical rainforest descending from the escarpments on both sides of the valley into the deep shadowed gullies. Other pockets of rainforest were surrounded by small trees and grassland, almost as if they had been deliberately landscaped. The thunderous noise from the falls blocked out all other sounds. The sky was overcast with low, rain-filled clouds, and though it was cooler up here, it was still hot and muggy.

Travelling a little further on, we passed the turnoff to the Varirata National Park, but we didn't have time to visit it. Soon we reached the Laloki River and the third bridge across it. Early in the war, engineers built a low-level steel and concrete structure which still remains today. This was the site of Ian Loudon's accident. On crossing this bridge, we stopped to view the Kokoda Trail Monument, a simple stone cairn. We then bumped and wound our way through undulating hills, lightly wooded with small trees and banksias, to Owers' Corner. Most of the once thickly forested hills I remembered had been cleared over the years for communal gardens. People still grow a wide range of tropical fruit and vegetables for themselves and to sell at village markets.

We drove on through Sogeri, a formerly thriving town that used to host agricultural shows, sports events and gymkhanas. Now, apart from the primary school, we could only see a couple of roadside stalls selling tropical fruit and vegetables. There were other buildings, but our limited time prevented further exploration. Graham was only familiar with the road to Sogeri, but with the help of a detailed map, we guided him onto a narrow, dirt track with deep potholes and washouts. I thought it more like a creek bed than a road. Graham was gripping the steering wheel and saying at frequent intervals, 'We'll have to turn back, the road is too bad.'

The four-wheel-drive was barely managing the huge potholes. If it had been raining, the unsealed road would have been impassable. During the plantation days, the managers kept this road graded and in good condition. Repairs were constant due to the regular heavy rains washing it out.

'It's not far,' we encouraged him.

'Let's go a little further.'

Around gentle, twisting bends of the open grassland, we drove the route I used to travel every day to primary school.

'Do you remember this?' Graham kept asking and looking at me to see my reaction. I did, and I didn't. It felt and looked familiar, yet strange at times. There were more houses now, and the landscape looked open and less covered than the landscape of my memories.

We passed the old Mororo plantation on the left, and I could just see a house on a hill in the distance. Perhaps it was the same one my father had built, but I couldn't be sure. A few kilometres on, we approached Eilogo. It had taken us about an hour to get here. We could see the tops of the rubber trees through the thick jungle plants which had reclaimed the land. Apart from a fruit seller at Sogeri, we hadn't seen any other people or vehicles.

On reaching Eilogo homestead, Graham parked the car and a young couple appeared with half a dozen children. Graham spoke to them in Motu, explaining why we were there, and asked if it was alright for us to look around and take photos. The couple were extremely welcoming and happy to show me around. The children looked unsure and hung back but still seemed keen to find out what was happening.

The terraced gardens my mother had planted and tended were long gone and replaced with long grass. I had expected this from social media posts of other expats who had gone back to their childhood homes and reported what they'd seen. But everything about the house felt familiar. The dining room had been portioned off with tin sheeting to create an extra room. I couldn't see into the bedrooms, as they had been rented out and had locks on them. The concrete floor surrounding a central courtyard where we used to ride our bikes still looked freshly polished. The teak pillars holding the roof seemed sturdy enough to last a hundred years.

The courtyard, still open to the sky, used to have a garden full of ferns and orchids. During heavy storms and torrential rain, those concrete floors would become small rivers as the rain pelted down in centimetres. The kitchen, now a shell, still had the remnants of the wood stove my mother cooked on. The tub and toilet in the bathroom were still in place, but no longer in use, as the room was being used for storage.

Memories flooded back. I remembered one evening when my sister locked the door, and she, my brother and I (who all shared the bath) slid across the concrete floor on our bare bums, getting up and running back to the tub to push off and repeat it. It was fun until my mother insisted the door be unlocked. I also remembered coming off my bike and hitting my head on the corner of a concrete plinth. The gash needed stitches, but because we were so far from a hospital, my mother spent the night holding the two pieces of skin together until they knitted.

This is where I was born and raised, and though the sense of familiarity was strong, the house no longer had any sense of home. I left feeling contented and grateful for the opportunity to revisit the centre of so many of my childhood memories.

Eilogo house, 2018

Postcript

In September 1959, the administration of Eilogo, Catalina and Mororo estates was reorganised, and the three individual businesses were amalgamated as Eilogo Estate Limited. The overall administration of the new company became the responsibility of Culver Matley, who would continue to run Eilogo, with Mr Graham Buckley as an assistant. Catalina estate would be supervised by John Lukin, where the main work required was repairing fences, the upkeep of stock and pastures, and the preparation of one hundred acres for rubber planting. Mr Cronan was assigned to supervise Mororo, where the main activity would be new clearing and planting for rubber.

Culver's resignation was dealt with at a company board meeting in May 1967. The position of manager was offered to John Lukin, who would take over the house at Eilogo. The company agreed to buy any furniture the Matley family did not wish to take to Australia and would continue to pay life insurance premiums for Culver until he turned sixty. The price of rubber had fallen dramatically, and the business overall had become unprofitable, so it was agreed the company should be sold if possible. Failing that, activities would be limited to the known profitable areas for tapping rubber.

In August 1978, the company's property, with all buildings, plant and machinery, was sold to the PNG Department of Lands, Survey and Environment for 72,000 kina. The company was placed into voluntary liquidation and subsequently wound up. After outstanding debtor and creditor accounts were finalised, the shareholders were left with 76,788 kina. At the time, this was equivalent to A$97,520, hardly a large reward for the decades of work put in by the planters.

The PNG government transferred Eilogo and other properties to the National Plantation Management Agency in late 1978. The Koiari people were encouraged to form the Sogeri Rubber Development Corporation and to borrow money to upgrade machinery and bulldoze old rubber trees. Like the planters who came before them, the Koiari were to be disappointed with the returns they received from the plantations.

Jack Matley died in 1958, and Martha Matley in 1969, in Saskatoon, Canada.

David Anderson died in 1971, and Florence Anderson in 1972, in Horsham, Victoria.

Culver Matley died in 1990, and Margaret Matley in 2007, in Victoria. Both Culver and Margaret's ashes were scattered at St John's Anglican Church, Portarlington.

Acknowledgements

My father burnt most of his papers when he was diagnosed with leukaemia, except a few business records that were saved. Fortunately, he was a keen photographer and left a historical trail with his photos. My mother was a prolific letter writer, and I gleaned much detail from her letters. I used my own and my family's personal knowledge and memories of how we lived and the events that took place.

Huge gratitude and thanks go to my fellow researcher Peter McCarthy. Without his encouragement and assistance, this book wouldn't have been finalised.

Barbara Barkley (nee Johnston), for her readiness in answering my questions.
Iris Clark, for relating some of the stories Martha Matley told her.
Amy Coburn.
Judy Connolly, (nee Johnston), for her readiness in answering my questions.
Reverend Mark J Dunn, retired Army chaplain, for putting me in touch with Bob Prewett, an expert in military history.
John Gill, who provided letters his father wrote on his time at Sogeri for cross-referencing.
Therese Horn, who read a later draft. Therese is a prolific reader, and getting her positive feedback was encouraging.

Kangan Institute teachers of the Professional Writing and Editing course: Peter Wiseman, Dr Ian Irvine, and Tru Dowling. These teachers were fantastic. They gave me the skills and confidence to put my story idea down on paper.

Cate Kennedy, for her insights and encouragement at the Words in Winter writing workshop.

Christina Matley, for her patience with my constant questions and probing of her memories of our time in Papua.

John Matley, for emailing a pdf of the Official Souvenir History of 2/9 Australian Field Regiment 1940-1945 so I could follow our father's journey in the Middle East.

Peter McCarthy, is an avid researcher. Though we both researched, I admit he did the heavy lifting. The number of times I nearly gave up, Peter would leap onto his computer, find something unique to push me along and inspire me. He also helped shape the story and spent many hours listening to my perceived 'roadblocks' and always found a way around them.

William (Bill) McGrath, (deceased), contacted me after recognising my name when I purchased a book from his online bookshop. He'd met my parents at Sogeri and remembered them with fondness. I was at a low point, and I took this as a sign I should keep going.

Jan Murray, for her patience in answering my constant questions and pointing me to the National Library to obtain a copy of *The Papua Club*.

Jenny Nestor.

Bob Prewett, was especially helpful and generous with his time, reviewing the War Years chapter for clarity and fact checking.

Katherine Seppings, of Sevenpens Publishing, helped this book come alive. Katherine read one of the earliest drafts and offered editing advice. Even though the book was still in its infancy, she encouraged me to continue with it. She read the final draft and offered invaluable suggestions. She also provided valuable advice regarding the referencing. Thank you, Katherine.

Bernard Schultz, for his exceptional proofreading and attention to detail skills. This work was read by many editing eyes and Bernard still managed to pick up what others missed. Thank you, Bernie.

Gavan Thomson.

Meredith Trewin-Shaw, for making available her mother's letters.

Iain White.

Smiley Williams,

Word Mine group members: Katherina Rapp, Rosie McKenry, Tricia O'Hara, Barbara Ashworth, and Ann de Hugard. Especially to Barb Ashworth for introducing me to these feisty, talented women. They read every form of this story and offered encouragement and editing advice.

Notes

Abbreviations:

BT   *Between the Touchwoods*, compiled and published by Punnichy and Districts History Book Committee, Punnichy, Canada, 1983.

HPN   *Handbook of Papua New Guinea*, First Edition, compiled and edited by Robson, RW, F.R.G.S. Pacific Publications Pty. Ltd., 1954.

OFSH   *Official Souvenir History of 2/9 Aust Field Regiment RAA Australian Imperial Forces, 1940-1945*, compiled by Glover EW, published by R Bale (CO) for the 2/9 Australian Field Regiment, 1945.

PC   Sinclair, J, *The Papua Club est. 1912: A History*, Crawford House Publishing, Adelaide, 2002.

PD   Lewis, DC, *The Plantation Dream: Developing British New Guinea and Papua, 1884-1942*, The Journal of Pacific History, c/o Division of Pacific and Asian History, Research School of Pacific and Asian Studies, Australian National University, Canberra, 1996.

PMTB   Hawthorne, S, *Port Moresby: Taim bipo*, Boolarong Press, Qld, 2011

PMYT   Stuart, I, *Port Moresby, yesterday and today*, Pacific Publications Pty Ltd, Sydney Australia, 1970.

SR   Taylor, L, *Snake Road: a guide to the history, people, and places of the Sogeri district*, Sogeri Publications, Sogeri National High School, Boroka, PNG, 1992.

Introduction

Flora and fauna of the Sogeri Plateau: Taylor, L, Snake Road (SR), p. 128.

Varirata National Park is described in: www.papuanewguinea. travel/varirata-national-park

The Kokoda Track and Owen Stanley Ranges environment of the Koiari and Orokaiva peoples is described in a UNESCO World Heritage Convention Tentative List at: https://whc.unesco.org/en/tentativelists/5061/

The leasing of Koiari land for planting rubber: Lewis, DC, *The Plantation Dream* (PD), p. 74.

The Australian Government arranging importation of rubber seeds: *Handbook of Papua New Guinea*, (HPN), p. 55.

The expectations of settlers on plantations: *The Plantation Dream* (PD), p. 245.

The fluctuating value of rubber: *Handbook of Papua New Guinea* (HPN), p. 57.

Rubber production during the war: 'Papuan Rubber Back in Production' *The Daily News* (Perth, WA), 19 February 1943, p. 4.

The National Plantations Management Agency in the 1970s: 'Bouncing Back', *Papua New Guinea Post-Courier* (Port Moresby), 17 October 1980, p. 23.

Early Life in Canada 1905 – 1935

The Matley family in Bramshott: https://cwleadbeater.wordpress.com/2016/10/16/the-matley-account-of-bramshott/

The life of Charles W. Leadbeater:
https://theosophy.wiki/en/Charles_Webster_Leadbeater

Details of the lives of Jack and Martha Matley in England come from family archives.

Settling on the prairies: Friesen, G, 'History of Settlement in the Canadian Prairies', *The Canadian Encyclopedia*, 23 December 2019, https://www.thecanadianencyclopedia.ca/en/article/prairie-west

Attracting British settlers to the prairies: Chandler, G, 'Selling the Prairie Good Life' originally appeared in the August-September 2006 issue of *The Beaver*, 7 September 2016, https://www.canadashistory.ca/explore/settlement-immigration/selling-the-prairie-good-life

John and Martha Matley as boarders with the Glover family: 1906 Canadian Census.

Treaty 4 — also known as the Qu'Appelle Treaty—was signed on 15 September 1874 at Fort Qu'Appelle, Saskatchewan.
In exchange for payments, provisions and rights to reserve lands, Treaty 4 ceded Indigenous territory to the federal government. The majority of Treaty 4 lands are in present-day southern Saskatchewan. Small portions are in western Manitoba and southern Alberta:
https://www.thecanadianencyclopedia.ca/en/article/treaty-4#:

The story of the prairie uprising: 'Taking the West—The North West Rebellion', *Le Canada, a People's History*, https://www.cbc.ca/history/SECTIONSE1EP10CH4LE.html

To earn title to his land grant, Arthur John Matley was required to report his activities from 1906 to 1910 to the Department of the

Interior in a statutory declaration, supported by sworn statements from two neighbours. This included land cleared, crops planted, buildings erected and so on. Copies were obtained from the Provincial Archives of Saskatchewan on 6 August 2019.

Background to life on the prairie: Salloum, H, 'Ploughing the Virgin Canadian Prairie', *Arab America*, 17 July 2019. https://www.arabamerica.com/plowing-the-virgin-canadian-prairie/

The story of the pink umbrella incident was passed down through the family.

In 1936, Jack and Martha Matley travelled to France for the unveiling of the Canadian War Memorial at Vimy Ridge. Jack was one of 6,000 Canadian ex-servicemen who attended the ceremony. For the story of the battle: Cook T, 'The Battle of Vimy Ridge, 9-12 April 1917', Canadian War Museum, 2023 https://www.warmuseum.ca/the-battle-of-vimy-ridge

Jack's letter about the death of his comrade: *Edmonton Journal*, Alberta, Canada, 16 June 1917, p. 9.

AA Beattie's poem: *Brandon's Military Museum Newsletter* Volume 3, Issue 3, July 2014, p 1.

Descriptions of Punnichy and the school based on: *Between the Touchwoods* (BT).

The story of the silk trains: Chandler, G, 'Canada's Silk Road', *Canada's History*, 17 August 2015, https://www.canadashistory.ca/explore/transportation/canada-s-silk-road

The Canadian droughts of the 1930s: Dyck, B, 'Dirty Thirties: Fact and Myth', *The Western Producer* 28 July 2005, https://www.producer.com/news/dirty-thirties-fact-and-myth/

Quotation about darkness at noon: Waiser, B, 'History Matters: Drought and dust a legacy of Great Depression' *Saskatoon Star Phoenix*, 21 November 2017, https://thestarphoenix.com/opinion/columnists/history-matters-drought-and-dust-a-legacy-of-great-depression

The effects of the drought and the relief efforts: *Saskatoon Star Phoenix*, 8 June 1965, p. 19.

My New Life Begins: Samarai Island & Papua 1935

Culver's farewell party: *Saskatoon Star Phoenix*, 7 September 1935, p.17.

Renovations to Aorangi: 'RMS Aorangi', *The Mercury* (Hobart, Tasmania), 7 November 1935, p. 2.

Description of the Monowai:
http://ssmaritime.com/Monowai.htm

Details of the Montoro:
https://www.clydeships.co.uk/view.php?ref=4413

The description of the journey to Samarai is based on: 'A South Seas Cruise', *The Sydney Morning Herald* (NSW), 19 September 1931, p. 9.

Poetic description of the islands: Osborne, C, 'New Guinea was once my home', *The Daily News* (Perth, WA), 19 September 1942, p. 15.

Description of Samarai: 'Samarai', *The Northern Miner* (Charters Towers, Qld), 30 September 1933, p. 3.

Samarai swimming baths: 'Samarai Notes', *Papuan Courier* (Port Moresby, PNG), 1 December 1939, p. 4.

The role of Samarai for the plantations: Osborne, C, 'New Guinea was once my home', *The Daily News* (Perth, WA), 19 September 1942, p. 15.

In 1935, former journalist Jessie Downie, James Matley's sister-in-law, stayed at Waigani plantation and described life there on her return to Perth: 'Life in Tropical New Guinea', *The Daily News* (Perth, WA), 9 July 1935, p. 8.

Loudon the uncrowned king of Papua: *The Plantation Dream* (PD), p. 187.

The weather and the capsized ketch: 'Papuan Notes', *Cairns Post* (Qld), 25 July 1936, p. 13.

Pre-War: Mororo & Eilogo 1936

Description of Eilogo estate: Taylor, J, 'Jeepers', *Pacific Islands Monthly*, 18 Nov 1946, p. 38-39.

Failure of the Eilogo coffee venture: *The Plantation Dream* (PD), p. 240.

The Eilogo airstrip: 'New Eilogo Drome. Further Advance In Commercial Aviation', *Papuan Courier* (Port Moresby, PNG), 1 July 1938, p. 7.

War Years: Middle East 1941

Culver's assignments and movements are taken from his service records, found in the National Archives of Australia: https://www.naa.gov.au/explore-collection/defence-and-war-service-records

The descriptions of departure from Sydney and arrival in Palestine are based on: *Official Souvenir History* (OFSH).

The description of the journey to the Middle East is based on diaries kept by Jim Long, a shoe store worker from Bendigo, who sailed on the Queen Elizabeth in September 1941: The Ash Long Collection - Jim Long's War Years, http://long.com.au/wordpress/?page_id=302

Living conditions in the desert: Official Souvenir History (OFSH).

Visit to Cairo: *The Ash Long Collection—Jim Long's War Years* http://long.com.au/wordpress/?page_id=302

The activities of a Light Aid Detachment were described by a war correspondent: Hetherington, J, 'Diggers build cars from scrap in the desert', *The Sun* (Sydney, NSW), 28 September 1941, p. 7.

Culver's war wound was a serious scar that we knew as children but was an accident as described. It is reported in his service record.

Regimental and LAD movements: *Official Souvenir History* (OFSH).

War Years: Return to Australia and Papua New Guinea 1942

Aspects of the return voyage to Australia from the Middle East in early 1942 on the *Duke of Athens*: Griffiths, G, 'Ships—The Duke of Athens', Cavalry News 46, November 1990, *2/6 Cavalry Commando Regiment and 2nd Cavalry Regiment* https://www.26cavcommando.org.au/index.php?option=com_cont ent&task=view&id=2611&Itemid=74&limit=1&limitstart=3

Movements of the LAD in Australia come from: *Official Souvenir History* (OFSH).

The dates of Culver's illness in Adelaide are in his service records.

Port Moresby 1943

The need for rubber was so acute that *the planters have been instructed to produce rubber to the fullest resources of the territory, irrespective of any damage or detriment to the future of the trees*: 'Rubber from New Guinea Again', *Newcastle Morning Herald and Miners' Advocate* (NSW), 3 January 1944, p. 3.

The large Japanese raid on Port Moresby: '100 Jap Planes Raid Port Moresby', *Narrandera Argus and Riverina Advertiser* (NSW), 16 April 1943, p. 3.

Evacuation of Port Moresby: 'New Guinea', *Townsville Daily Bulletin* (Qld), 11 March 1942, p. 7.

The market garden schemes: 'Fresh Vegetables at Port Moresby', *Rutherglen Sun and Chiltern Valley Advertiser* (Vic), 6 October 1942, p. 9.

Death of Bluey Truscott: National Archives of Australia, NAA:A705, 166/40/

Use of planation houses as hospitals: 'Home Again', *The Age* (Melbourne, Vic), 11 July 1945, p. 4.

Output of the gardens: *Snake Road* (SR), p. 36.

Army Service Headquarters: *Snake Road* (SR), p. 39.

Work gangs and mosquitoes: Hutton G, 'Port Moresby – A Changed Town', *Nambour Chronicle and North Coast Advertiser* (Qld), 26 February 1943, p. 5.

Collecting latex: Taylor, J, 'Jeepers', *Pacific Islands Monthly*, 18 Nov 1946, p. 38-39.

Rubber production and costs: 'Papuan Rubber', *Nambour Chronicle and North Coast Advertiser* (Qld), 8 June 1951, p. 4.

The crash of the Catalina: https://pacificwrecks.com/aircraft/pby/2447.html

Port Moresby 1945

Administration and the Production Control Board: 'Future Control in New Guinea', *Townsville Daily Bulletin* (Qld), 30 December 1944, p. 4.

New Beginnings 1946

The Trusteeship Agreement and the New Guinea mandate: Hutton G, 'Our New Guinea Record and Future Tasks', *The Argus* (Melbourne), 27 December 1946, p. 2.

Margaret's letter of acceptance survives in the family archive.

A description of the wedding: 'Country Weddings', *The Argus* (Melbourne), 18 February 1947, p. 10.

Mororo 1948

Pit sawing: 'The Days of the Pit-Saw', *The Advertiser* (Adelaide), 16 February 1935, p. 11.

The incident with Igua: 'Port Moresby News', *The Telegraph* (Brisbane, Qld), 15 Feb 1938, p. 11.

Stanley Cuthbert Wigley MB, BS, FRCP: 'Vale September 2000', The Papua New Guinea Association of Australia. https://pngaa.org/vale-september-2000/#Wigley

Dr John Gunther: Nelson, HN, 'Sir John Thomson Gunther (1910–1984)', *The Australian Dictionary of Biography* Volume 17, 2007. https://adb.anu.edu.au/biography/gunther-sir-john-thomson-12574/text22641

Mororo 1949

The busy wharf at Port Moresby: 'Industry Revived In New Guinea', *The Advertiser* (Adelaide, SA), 23 August 1947, p. 11.
Doctor Joan Refshauge: Denoon, D, 'Joan Janet Brown Refshauge (1906–1979)', *The Australian Dictionary of Biography* Volume 16, 2002. https://adb.anu.edu.au/biography/refshauge-joan-janet-brown-11497/text20507

The incident between the Rigo and the Tufi: 'Tribal Battle Frustrated', *Singleton Argus* (NSW), 8 July 1949, p. 5.

Mary's visit to Mororo during Culver's recruiting trip: Letters Mary wrote to her mother, family archives.

Social Life 1950s

The first Sogeri Agricultural Show: 'First Agricultural Show', *Papuan Times* (PNG), 30 July 1953, p. 6.

David Crawley: 'People - David Crawley MBE - Bandmaster, European Constabulary, New Guinea Police Force, Founder of the New Guinea Police Force Band', *Lost Lives* https://www.jje.info/lostlives/people/crawleyd.html

Schooling at Sogeri: *Snake Road* (SR), p. 242.

Primary A and Primary T schools: *The Handbook of Papua and New Guinea*, 5th Edition, p. 193. (HPN)

The fight on Koitaki plantation: 'Goilala and Chimbu Fight', *Papuan Times* (PNG), 25 July 1952, p. 1.

The Papua Club and Planters' Association

Origins of the Planters' Association and the Papua Club: Sinclair J, *The Papua Club est. 1912: A History,* Crawford House Publishing, Adelaide, 2002.

Dress code for the Papua Club: *The Plantation Dream* (PD), p. 261. Political considerations, the low price paid for rubber and the lack of village life on the plantations: 'Rubber planters in Papua face a crisis', *The Daily Telegraph* (Sydney, NSW), 20 April 1954, p. 19.

Sir Paul Hasluck: Allbrook, M, 'Sir Paul Meernaa Hasluck (1905–1993)', *The Australian Dictionary of Biography* Volume 19, 2021. https://adb.anu.edu.au/biography/hasluck-sir-paul-meer-naa-18555

The American hydrogen bomb: 'Potency of Hydrogen Bomb', *Maryborough Chronicle* (Qld), 19 February 1954, p. 1. Air-freighting cattle for Eilogo: 'Air-freighting Cattle to New Guinea', Balonne Beacon (St. George, Qld), 3 February 1955, p. 1.

Air-freighting cattle for Eilogo: 'Beef Cattle Flown from R'ton to New Guinea', *The Central Queensland Herald* (Rockhampton, Qld), 20 January 1955, p. 10.

Prince Philip at the Koitaki Club: Fitzgerald, M, 'Everyone Asks What's the Duke Really Like', *The Argus* (Melbourne), 26 November 1956, p. 8.

Back to Canada

The high cost of living in PNG: 'We Grumble Too Much', *The Horsham Times* (Vic.), 10 March 1953, p. 3.

Margaret's life in PNG: 'Only White Woman on New Guinea Rubber Plantation', *The Horsham Times* (Vic), 22 July 1957, p. 5.

The Constellation aircraft: 'How the Constellation Became the Star of the Skies', *Lockheed Martin Corporation*, 1 October 2020. https://www.lockheedmartin.com/en-us/news/features/history/constellation.html

Eilogo Plantation 1957 – 1966

The Redex trial: 'Redex wrecks tear on', *The Argus* (Melbourne, Vic), 26 August 1955, p. 5.

Ernie Kriewald's entry in the Redex trial:
'New Guinea Trial Entry', *The Cumberland Argus* (Parramatta, NSW), 25 May 1955, p. 2.

Woody and her hotel: 'My hat! Woody's leaving us — and she means it', *Papua New Guinea Post-Courier* (Port Moresby), 4 February 1975, p. 5.

The evacuation of West Irian: 'Dutch Planning Evacuation: West NG under UN in 4 months', *The Canberra Times* (ACT), 3 August 1962, p. 1.

The quotation on the offense of playing cards came from:
'NG Cards Law to Stay', *The Canberra Times* (ACT), 25 November 1965, p. 24.

The statement by the Minister for Territories, Mr Barnes, came from: 'Can We Give Papua A Choice?', *The Canberra Times* (ACT), 29 May 1965, p. 2.

Bibliography

Primary Sources:

Private letters and photos of Culver and Margaret Matley.

Hawthorne, Stuart, *Port Moresby (Taim bipo)*, Boolarong Press, Qld, 2011

Lewis, DC, *The Plantation Dream: Developing British New Guinea and Papua, 1884-1942*, The Journal of Pacific History, c/o Division of Pacific and Asian History, Research School of Pacific and Asian Studies, Australian National University, Canberra, 1996

Between the Touchwoods, compiled and published by Punnichy and Districts History Book Committee, Punnichy, Canada, 1983

Sinclair, James, *The Papua Club est. 1912: A History*, Crawford House Publishing, Adelaide, 2002.

Stuart, Ian, *Port Moresby, yesterday and today*, The Sydney & Melbourne Publishing Co. Pty. Ltd., 1970

Taylor, Lance, *Snake Road: a guide to the history, people, and places of the Sogeri district*, Sogeri Publications, Sogeri National High School, Boroka, PNG, 1992

Online Sources:

Canada's History www.canadahistory.ca

Canadian War Museum

https://www.warmuseum.ca/the-battle-of-vimy-ridge

2/6 Cavalry Commando Regiment Association
https://26cavcommando.org.au

The Ash Long Collection
https://long.com.au/wordpress/?page_id=302

'History of Settlement in the Canadian Prairies',
The Canadian Encyclopedia, The Government of Canada
https://www.thecanadianencyclopedia.ca/en

https://www.lockheedmartin.com/enus/news/features/history/constellation.html

Provincial Archives of Saskatchewan
https://www.saskarchives.com/

Digitised copies of *The Papuan Courier*, *Nambour Chronicle* and *North Coast Advertiser*, *Pacific Islands Monthly* and *Cairns Post*, https://trove.nla.gov.au/newspaper/

List of photographs and maps

About the Author
Swimming in Eilogo Creek, 1963 -
Photo by Culver Matley

Preface
The Matley family at Eilogo, 1964 -
Photographer unknown

Timeline of events
Arthur (Jack) Matley Volunteer 2nd Kent Garrison Artillery
(1900) - Photographer unknown

Introduction
Map of Indonesia, PNG, Australia - Green Graphics
Map of The Sogeri Plateau, PNG - Green Graphics

Early Life in Canada 1905 – 1935
Culver Matley in hockey gear, Punnichy, Canada, 1930s -
Photographer unknown
Punnichy, Saskatchewan, Canada 1930s -
Photographer unknown
Arthur (Jack) and Martha Matley, prior to emigration,
Croydon, England - Photographer unknown
Martha holding baby Francis, Brandon Manitoba 1906 -
Photographer unknown

James (Jim) Matley on a visit to Canada (1907) - Photographer unknown

Francis, Culver, Arthur (jnr.), Martha and Mary Matley, 1914 Photographer unknown

Culver, Mary, Francis, Martha, Arthur jnr. 1930s - Photographer unknown

Tepees, Punnichy, 1930s - Photographer unknown

My New Life Begins: Samarai Island & Papua 1935

Map of Samarai, PNG - Green Graphics

Buildings and the jetty at Samarai, Papua New Guinea, ca. 1927 - State Library of Queensland

Street view on Samarai Island, ca. 1905 - State Library of Queensland

James (Jim) Matley - Photographer unknown

Pre-War: Mororo & Eilogo 1936

Rouna Falls mid-1950s - Photo by C Matley

Rubber tapping and drying - Photo by C Matley

Clearing for rubber plantation (x4) - Photos by C Matley

War Years: Middle East 1941

68 Light Aid Detachment - Photographer unknown

Culver in uniform, 1942 - Photographer unknown

Dawn Patrol, Culver on right, 1942 - Photographer unknown

A field gun 1942 - Photographer unknown

Culver (second from right) with friends 1942 - Photographer unknown

Living conditions 1942 - Photographer unknown

Baalbek, Lebanon. Culver on right, 1942 -
Photographer unknown

War Years: Return to Australia and Papua New Guinea 1942
Culver on right, 1942 - Photographer unknown
Culver on right, with LAD truck, 1942 -
Photographer unknown

Port Moresby 1943
Culver on left, hotel lunch 1943 - Photographer unknown
Cattle at Catalina - Photographer unknown

Port Moresby 1945
Margaret Anderson (Geelong Hospital, 1939) -
Photographer unknown

New Beginnings 1946
Culver and Margaret Matley's wedding, Presbyterian Church,
Horsham, 1947 - Photographer unknown

Papua New Guinea: Mororo Plantation 1947
Margaret at Hombrom Bluff, PNG - Photo by C Matley

Mororo 1948
Matley home, Mororo - Photo by C Matley

Margaret's Story
Margaret Anderson - Photographer unknown

Mororo 1949
Mororo, PNG - Photo by C Matley

Tribal Matters
Worker tapping rubber - Photo by C Matley
Eilogo River flooding - Photo by C Matley

Culver's Story
Culver on a boat to a local island near Port Moresby -
Photographer unknown

The Papua Club and Planters' Association
Plantation Managers: Don Malcolm, Lisle Johnston, Brian
Lukin, Culver Matley - Photographer unknown
HRH The Duke of Edinburgh at the Koitaki Club 1955 -
Photographer unknown

Back to Canada
Margaret and Beth at Mororo - Photo by C Matley
QANTAS Connie aeroplane prior to departure, 1957 -
Photo by C Matley
Francis, Mary, Arthur (Jack), Martha and Culver Matley
1957 - Photographer unknown

Eilogo Plantation 1957 – 1966
Creek crossing Sogeri district - Photo by C Matley
Anthea and nurse girl holding John in the garden, Eilogo -
Photo by C Matley
Margaret on Moresby wharf 1962 - Photo by C Matley

Life at Eilogo

Matley home, Eilogo - Photo by C Matley

Margaret in the centre garden at Eilogo - Photo by C Matley

In the garden at Eilogo (Culver with John, Christina and Anthea) - Photo by Margaret Matley

Gardener at Eilogo - Photo by Margaret Matley

Swimming pool at Koitaki Club - Photo by C Matley

Waiting for the plane to travel south to Australia, Port Moresby 1960 - Photo by C Matley

Anthea as the Yellow Rose of Texas at fancy dress party, Sogeri, 1960 - Photo by C Matley

Changes Afoot: Eilogo 1967

Rubber plant at Eilogo - Photo by C Matley

Rubber processing, Eilogo - Photo by C Matley

Latex vats at Eilogo - Photo by C Matley

Port Moresby 2018

Pacific Ocean, Port Moresby, PNG, 2018 -
Photo by Anthea Matley

Buildings of Port Moresby, 2018 -Photo by Anthea Matley

Eilogo house, 2018 - Photo by Anthea Matley